Mard Maratha

Tales of Unsung Warriors from Swarajya

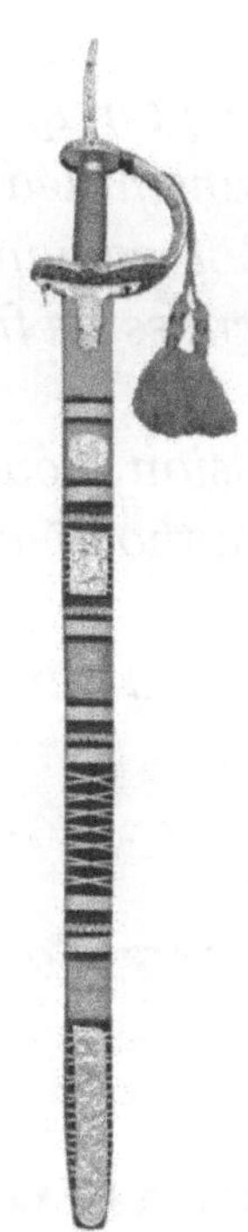

Gopish Gopalkrishna

www.redtoucanpublisher.com

First Edition, 2021

Requests for permission should be addressed to gopishtheauthor@gmail.com

ISBN - 978-93-92900-04-4

DEDICATED TO

All brave warriors who have given their lives to serve our Motherland
and
My Family

CONTENTS

ACKNOWLEDGMENTS

I would like to acknowledge all my readers for loving my first book *"Astavakra-The Vedic Sage"* which became Amazon best sellers. The book is doing well on all platforms. Thanks again for encouraging and motivating me.

With all your blessings, I am now coming with my second book, *"Mard Maratha-The Tales of Unsung Warriors from Swarajya."* My second book was bound to happen sooner or later, but the topic of Maratha warriors was accidental. All thanks to Mr. Ajay Devgan and his movie *"Tanhaji: The Unsung Warrior."* This film was released on January 10, 2020. This movie traced the life of Maratha warrior Tanhaji Malusare, where Tanhaji attempts to recapture the Kondhana fort from Udaybhan Singh Rathore, trusted guard of the Mughal emperor. It was an inspirational story and movie was amazing. When I watched this movie, I decided to explore the history of the Maratha empire and its warriors and write a book on it. I was then aware of only a few Maratha warriors named Chhatrapati Shivaji Maharaj and Baji Rao Peshwa. I was curious about the Maratha empire; our education system didn't detail our Indian warriors. Eventually, I started researching Maratha empire and Maratha warriors by reading books, blogs, articles, discussing with people associated with Maratha history. In this book, I tried to cover the entire period of the Maratha empire so that readers can know the journey of Marathas in Indian history.

This book is the outcome of research done by me in my capacity. Therefore, I am not challenging or questioning any Historians or Authors who may have different versions of the Maratha empire.

As always, I am thankful to my family for giving me unconditional love and support.

Credit for all sketches in this book goes to **Nabanita Das,** After my first book, it's my second collaboration with this fantastic Artist. **Sankhadip Sengupta,** an urban minstrel, chose music over IT. He helped with the background score for the promotional video. **Sonam Sharma** created the cover page for this book. She is marvelous designer. **Kunjal Asher** for creating a promotional video.

DISCLAIMER

This book is the outcome of research done by the author in his personal capacity. Hence not challenging or questioning any Historians or Authors who may have different versions of the Maratha Empire and Maratha warriors. Many chapters and stories in this book are the work of fiction. Unless otherwise indicated, all the names, characters, places, events, and incidents in this book are either the product of the information available in the public domain or used in a fictitious manner. Any similarity to actual individuals, alive or dead, or actual events is purely coincidental.

In addition, the publisher and the author assume no obligation for errors, imprecision, omissions, or any other inconsistencies herein. This book is meant as a source of valuable information from ancient India for the reader. However, it is not meant as an ancillary for any historical data.

The content of this book is for entertainment reading purposes only. It is not intended to make changes in any of the historical facts. Furthermore, this book is not intended to hurt any person (dead or alive), caste, community. Images used in the book are purely for making stories more relevant. They don't have any relevance to any real characters.

Chapter I
Ideology of "SWARAJYA"

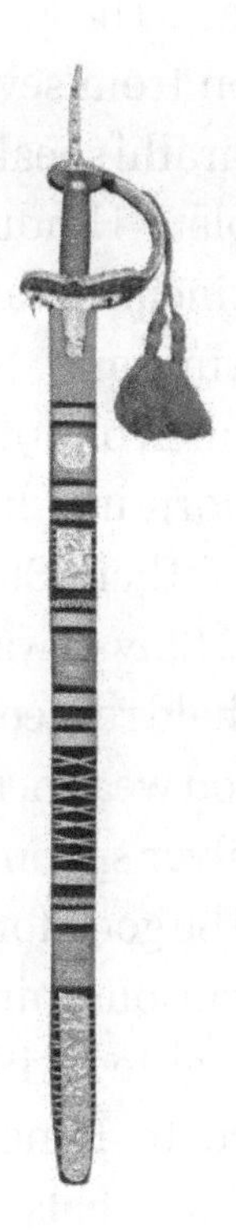

Swarajya means self - rule, not for individual benefit but to eradicate the injustice done by invaders and tyrant rulers.

The start of the 18th Century saw the meritorious emergence of a particular Marathi-speaking warrior group belonging originally to the Deccan plateau. This was the period when most of the Indian territory was ruled by Mughals. The Mughals struggled to maintain their power due to opposition from several regions throughout the Indian subcontinent. This Marathi speaking group shot to popularity due to their vision of complete Hindu Independence or Hindavi Swarajya. The roots of the principle Maratha ideology can be traced back to Shivaji's years of growing up.

Shivaji Bhosale took birth on 19th February 1630 in Shivner, Pune, Maharastra. He was born in a kingdom that was ruled by a dictator foreign ruler. His father, Shahaji Raje Bhosale, was a minister in Bijapur Sultanate. Shivaji was the second child of Shahaji and his wife, Jijabai. Shahaji held respectful positions and was from a wealthy family. He owned good wealth, land, and luxuries. So we can say Shivaji was born with a silver spoon in his mouth. With so much power and wealth, life should be good for anyone.

Shivaji's open spirit, curious mind, and courage to follow his instincts were virtues he was gifted with since early childhood. His wise mother, Jijabai, shifted to Pune by Shahaji after mutually agreeing on peace with the Mughals. Shivaji grew up under the influence of his mother's educated and courageous ideologies and the ethically prosperous supervision of the then administrator of Pune, Dadaji Konddeo. Although a very dedicated and disciplined student, Shivaji had his fair share of adventures, much to the displeasure of his mentor. Shivaji's close associations with the Maval children weren't controlled by his father. These associations ultimately contributed to several star Maratha warriors like Baji Prabhu Deshpande, Tanaji Malusare, and Shivaji's understanding of his future empire.

One of the significant reasons why Shivaji is one of the most celebrated warriors of the country was his military tactics. Besides war dexterity, Shivaji's ace was his expertise in his arena. Shivaji was a warrior who knew a land's most significant possessions are its natural resources. Therefore, he made sure to know his Kingdom like the back of his head. His childhood knowledge can be owed to his rendezvous with the Mavals, which was brilliantly used while strategizing any war in his territory.

Shivaji was very young when he started observing the atrocities that the Mughal powers put the general public through. Shivaji gained formal training as a warrior from his father, Shahaji. After that, his mind, beliefs, and opinions started shaping up, which finally gave birth to the ideology of complete freedom from the cruelty, unfair domination, and oppressive rule of external forces. He took the oath of Hindavi Swarajya which translated to the 'liberty and self-rule of the Indians'.

Based on the ideology of *Swarjaya,* Shivaji Maharaj started a mission of self-rule and established Maratha empire.

Importance of Raireshwar Temple

Raireshwar fort, situated in Bhor, around 80-90 KM from Pune, holds a special place in Maratha history. This is where Shivaji, in his early 20s, took an oath of "Swarajya" In 1645, Shivaji Maharaj decided to stand against the Mughals and fight for Independence. Along with his few friends, he visited the Raireshwar temple of Lord Shiva. This was the perfect place for rebellious activities. The Oath of Swarajya - Shivaji and his friends slit their thumbs and offered it on the Shiva Linga. With this, they took the oath of Independence and decided till their last breath, they will stand by Shivaji and fight for the decisive goal of Hindavi Swarajya.

Chapter 2
Maratha Empire
"THE BEGINNING"

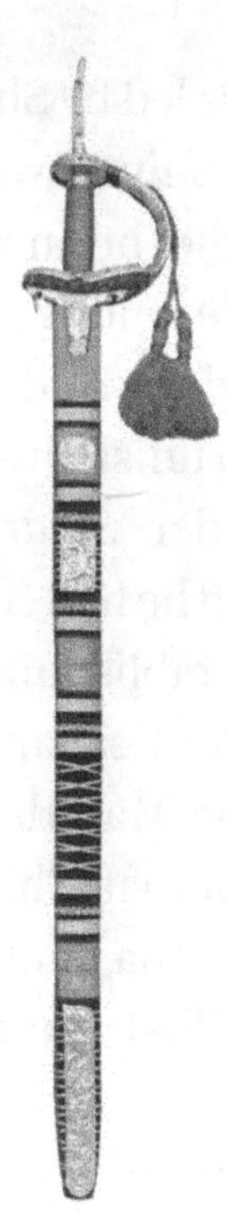

Maratha empire was founded by Chhatrapati Shivaji Maharaj. It dominated a large portion of *Bharat* (India) during the 17th and 18th Centuries. Formally the Maratha Empire began in 1674 with the rise of Chhatrapati Shivaji. Maratha empire is principally credited with the authentic Indian rulers who ended the Mughal rule in *Bharat.* During their peak, Maratha empire was extended from Peshawar (currently in Pakistan) in the North to Thanjavur (Tamil Nadu) in the South. Maratha empire's decadence occurred during the early 19th Century.

In 1645, Marathas were led by Shivaji, who protested the rule of the Sultanate of Bijapur. Shivaji was the visionary leader and master strategist. He was the brainchild of the term *"Hindavi Swarajya"* known for self-rule among the Hindus, with all religions having equal respect and rights. Under the leadership of Shivaji, Marathas were determined to finish the Mughal empire and wanted to bring the country ruling under "*Swarajya.*" However, Shivaji had conflicts with the Mughals, and he had created animosity towards the Mughals. Hence, the idea of establishing the Maratha kingdom came into Shivaji's mind. This idea of expanding the Hindu state in the subcontinent gave birth to the Maratha kingdom on June 6, 1674, under the leadership of Chhatrapati Shivaji. He was the first ruler of the Maratha empire. The Maratha empire was formally established with the coronation of their first Chhatrapati, Shivaji Maharaj, a marvelous figure in Indian history.

As soon as Shivaji became the supreme leader of the Maratha kingdom, he focused on expanding his territory. He made Raigad as capital of the Maratha Kingdom and captured parts like Athani, Ponda, Karwar, and Kolhapur. This was just the foundation of the expansion of the Maratha empire.

Shivaji fought for the freedom of the nation from invaders. His mission was to fight against foreign invaders and NOT against other specific religions.

The Maratha confederacy rose to be one of the most incredible powers in the subcontinent. They expanded their territories to most north and south regions to overthrow the Mughals at the center. After enormous victories and expansion, the empire declined due to internal battles and mismanagement among the Marathas that ultimately led to the defeat of Peshwa Baji Rao II at the hands of the Britishers.

This book is dedicated to all unsung warriors of the Maratha Kingdom. They not only played a critical role during Maratha's rule for its expansion but fought bravely with Mughals and Britishers and ensured the vision of Chhatrapati Shivaji is fulfilled. This is an account that traces the history of the Maratha empire through its peaks and falls.

It was not an easy path for Shivaji to establish a Kingdom of his own. It was an uphill task. Many historical changes happened during the journey of Shivaji Bhosale becoming Chhatrapati Shivaji Maharaj; the following chapters will take you through this incredible journey.

Chapter 3
Shivaji Bhosale
To
Chhatrapati Shivaji Maharaj

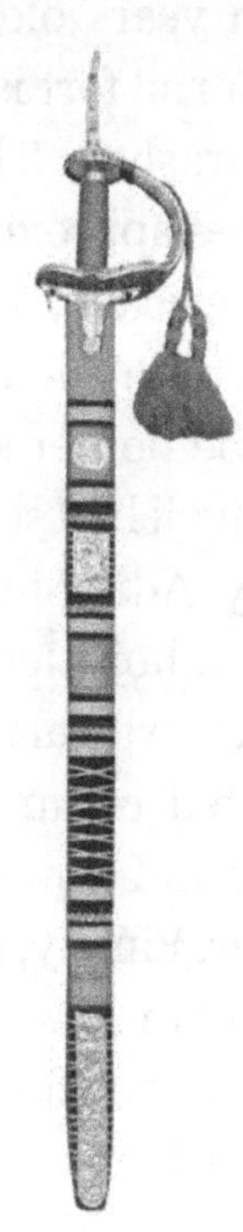

Shivaji's master plan of mutiny was weaved long back when he was hardly 15 years old. He started with what he came to be most popularly known for--capturing forts as a symbol of expanding power and Empire. The first fort he acquired can surprisingly not be credited to his bravery and battle skills but his shrewd and discerning diplomatic strategies. In his lifespan, Shivaji fought mainly with two significant powers, Adil Shahi, the seventh ruler of the Bijapur Sultanate, and Mughals.

The Bijapur forts of Torna and Kondana were acquired by Shivaji when he was sixteen years old. He used persuasion and bribing to achieve this feat. Torna fort is located at the very remote place of village Velhe in Maharashtra. This fort is located inside the dense forests of Sahyadri and at approximately 1,403 meters (4,603 ft) above sea level. So strategically, this fort didn't have much importance. Hence, Adil Shah didn't deploy much of the Army at this fort, thinking no one would be bothered to reach such height and capture the fort. However, Shivaji had strategically decided to attack forts with less attention by Adil Shah. He was supported by experienced commanders Kanhoji Jedhe, Sonopant Dabir, Baji Pasalkar, and other Deskmukhs who also believed in the ideology of *Swarajya*. So, with his trusted commanders, Shivaji planned to capture forts in remote places and slowly and steadily expanded his army and fortresses in number. Finally, in 1646 Shivaji captured the Torna fort, which became one of the first forts of the Maratha empire.

This event marked a silent declaration of a cold war between Shivaji and the Bijapur forces, which was duly predicted to grow into a full-blown battle by both powers. In 1648, Shahaji was arrested by the troops of Bijapur against the interests of Bijapur. Shahaji was taken to the Bijapur and forced to surrender the forts of Banglore and Kondana. When his father was captured, Shivaji first practiced his strategy that later became his classic. He stayed low and strategized, combining forces with diplomacy until his enemy lost his guard, released Shahaji, and he could go on the offensive. He applied different tactics while confronting significant Maratha powers under the service of Adil Shah. This resulted in the aggravation of the ruler of Bijapur. He, in desperation, sent his trusted General, Afzal Khan, in a bid to stifle Shivaji's consolidation, which ensued into one of the most revered battles that Shivaji fought.

Unfolding Sequence - Battle Of Pratapgadh

In 1649 Afzal Khan was the governor of Wai, which was next to the Jawali region. He always wanted to capture Jawali. However, before he could execute his plan, Shivaji Maharaj captured Jawali by defeating More's Army, who were rulers of Jawali. There were mainly two reasons why Shivaji wanted Jawali under his control. First, this area was in dense forest and was best for Guerilla warfare by Shivaji. Secondly, Jawali is located near the Arabic ocean, making it a perfect choice for Shivaji to expand *Swarajya's* Naval base. During the event of capturing Jawali, Shivaji killed Chandrarao More, one of the rulers of Jawali.

After few years of the above incident, Prataprao More, the brother of Chandrarao More, joined hands with Afzal Khan to defeat Shivaji. They decided to start their campaign against Marathas by winning back Jawali first. Strategically also Jawali was an important region for Afzal Khan. Shivaji was always prepared for this attack; hence he moved south from Raigad Maratha capital to Jawali. This is because a more significant part of the Kingdom in the northern region will be free from warfare stress. Keeping a base in Jawali also helped Shivaji keep a close eye on any movement by Afzal Khan. Shivaji was prepared for a decisive battle since he conquered Jawali. For this he constructed the Pratapgadh fort around 3 years before Afzal Khan campaigned against Marathas.

The battle of Pratapgadh is one of those that Marathas hold with high esteem and was a transcendent victory of Shivaji. Fought on the foothills of the Pratapgadh fort, Shivaji had seen this battle a long way coming and was prepared to give a massive response to his enemies. Adil Shahi forces were on a savage offensive, destroying Hindu temples and holy places, raiding and killing people. And finally forcing Shivaji to retreat to a brutal war. However, what Afzal Khan misunderstood to be a victory on the way, Shivaji upturned into his call for death and defeat. In the facade of a peace agreement, Shivaji met Afzal Khan to negotiate one on one, with only ten soldiers on standby. The combat escalated quickly into a bloody fight. Shivaji came more than prepared and used wise generalship to end the battle in favor of the Marathas and caused severe casualties, both for the army and the Adil Shahi pride.

Following the success of the Pratapgadh battle, Shivaji went on a rampage by seizing forts, raiding territories, overthrowing lesser powerful empires. These included several milestone events that involved Shivaji going back and forth as a military strategy adapting technique on several instances. One such event was the siege in Panhala, which was supposed to end with Shivaji handing over the fort in 1660, only to recapture in 1773. Such strategies were employed after careful consideration of enemy power and forces.

Adil Shah was desperate to eliminate Shivaji and sought help and formed alliances with every external power possible. The Mughals were ready to face the Marathas in the North while the British confronting Shivaji in the South. Hence leaving Shivaji with nothing but his loyal soldiers and his inventive military tactics to rely on. One famous and highly reminisced story is Shivaji's escape to Vishalgadh, and Baji Prabhu Deshpande's undeterred valor while fighting off the enemy keeps them away from his leader. I will cover this incident in detail in the upcoming chapters.

Shivaji's ultimate diplomatic tactics were proven when he managed to break his enemy's strength by joining hands with the greater enemies. Soon after defeating Adil Shah, Shivaji weighed his options and inferred that it was the right time to claim, Bijapur and *Swarajya*. This led to the Marathas' raids on Mughal territories starting in early 1657 from Ahmednagar. A furious Aurangzeb, the Mughal Emperor, began to set up his large troops of an army against Shivaji, who managed to defeat each opponent, one by one, if not sooner than later.

In the years building up to Shivaji's official coronation as the Maratha emperor or Chhatrapati, Shivaji got arrested in Agra, escaped unscathed, negotiated peace, and restocked his dwindling army and economy to take on the Mughals. Shivaji declared his aggressive strategy with a second raid on the wealthy port, Surat. Again, he braved the Mughals, Dutch and British counterparts. He responded to treacheries and attacks by capturing territories lost in the past years within months. During this phase, many Maratha warriors joined Shivaji for his dream of making the Maratha empire.

Chhatrapati

This word is derived from the Sanksrit word. "Chhatra" means Umbrella, and "Pati" means Master or Ruler. Hence, Chhatrapati is referred to a one who protects his subjects like an Umbrella.

Ganimi Kawa

This is a Marathi name for Guerilla warfare. Marathas used Ganimi Kawa to fight out their enemies. This is a form of war with military tactics carried out by small groups like paramilitary personnel or armed civilians. This includes raids, sabotages, ambushes hit and run tactics to fight against large and less-mobile traditional military.

Chapter 4
Tax System
"Chauth and Sardeshmukhi"

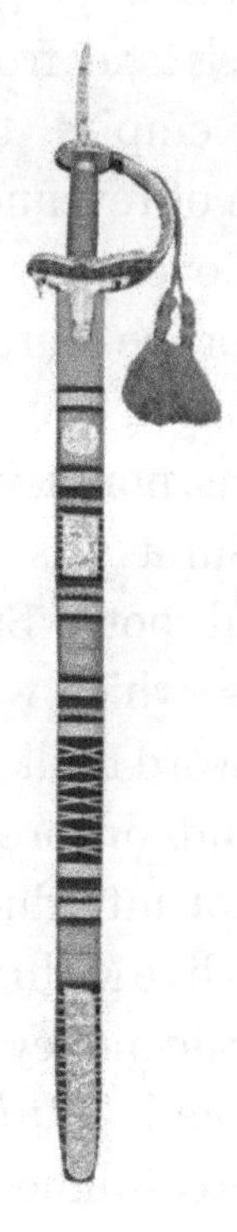

Before we go further to know about Maratha warriors, I would like to mention few details on the tax systems which were the reason for contention among different rulers during medieval times. Many believe it was purely a religion-based battle between Marathas, Adil Shahi, Mughals, British, and Portuguese. However, even though few rulers did use religion to appease many parts and regions. Their primary motive was to get most of their empire's taxes from nearby territory rulers.

During the Maratha empire, two sources of taxes were collected *Chauth* (one-fourth of revenue) and *Sardeshmukhi* (one-tenth of income for King/Governor). These two taxes were the primary sources of revenue for the Maratha administration. But the matter of fact is that both *Chauth* and *Sardeshmukhi* were not the sources of income for Marathas, nor they introduced these two taxes.

In 1664 and 1670, Surat was under the Mughal regime. Shivaji Maharaj attacked and looted Surat. These loots led to the revenue source for Marathas, which was called *"Mulkgiri,"* which was derived from the Arabic word Mulk means country, and *Griftan* (take), which meant looting raids on foreign lands.

"Mulkgiri" too was not introduced by Marathas. In India, initially, it was set by invaders like Mahmud Ghazni, Alauddin Khilji, etc. But, for Marathas, it was raid money from non Maratha land.

Later Shivaji replaced *"Mulkgiri"* with *Chauth* and *Sardeshmukhi*. However, this continued to be the constant source of revenue for decades to come.

By now, you should have got a fair knowledge of how Shivaji Maharaj became Chhatrapati and established an empire based on *Swarajya*. So, let's start the journey to know about the warriors of the Maratha empire. These unsung warriors contributed towards keeping the ideology of *Swarajya* high.

Chapter 5
Baji Pasalkar
"First Commander Of *Swarajya*"

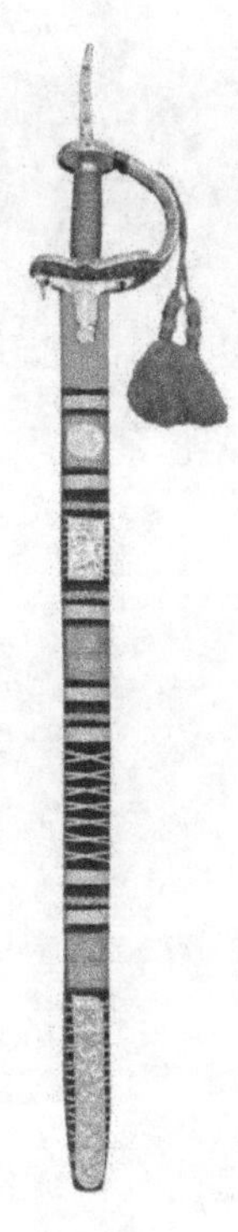

Baji Pasalkar was born in Mose Khore near Pune and was the Deshmukh of Maval province. He was the first commander in chief of *Swarajya*, even though he was one of the oldest warriors in the Maratha army, he was quickest and strongest. He was a strong left-leaning man with a robust body and a stubborn mustache. He played a critical part in formulating the ground army for Shivaji during the inception of *Swarajya*.

When the idea of *Swarajya* came into Shivaji's mind, he was looking for leaders who had a vision of *Swarajya* like him to build the empire. He needed an experienced and influencer leader who had a connection with many communities and tribes and influence the masses. During this time, he came to know about Baji Pasalkar. Shivaji personally wrote a letter to Baji Pasalkar and requested him to join the movement of *Swarajya*. When Baji Pasalkar received the letter from Shivaji, he was pleasantly surprised and happy to see the vision of a young boy at the age of sixteen. Baji Pasalkar also believed in the ideology of *Swarajya* and he went and met Shivaji in Pune. After meeting Shivaji, he promised Shivaji to extend all support for establishing the *Swarajya*. He knew if he supports Shivaji's movement, other people, communities, tribes will join him. Immediately he started contacting other Deshmukhs and other local leaders to join him and help Shivaji.

Within no time, Baji Pasalkar raised a large army for Shivaji and played a vital role in capturing the Torna fort that Shivaji won under the *Swarajya* movement. This victory sent a positive message across the region, and many Deshmukh and Sardars started joining Shivaji. When Adil Shah came to know about the influence of Shivaji in the region, he decided to attack Shivaji and finish the *Swarajya* movement. He sent Fateh Khan to attack Deccan to defeat Shivaji.

Shivaji has already calculated this movement in advance; news came to him that Fateh Khan is marching towards Purandhar fort. This was a crucial movement for *Swarajya*. If Fateh Khan attacks the Purandhar fort, it was a must for Shivaji to win the battle. He showed his faith and trust to Baji Pasalkar, considering the experience and leadership quality that Pasalkar possessed. Shivaji honored Baji Pasalkar as the first Senapati of the Maratha army to fight against Fateh Khan to protect Purandhar fort.

Fateh Khan and his large army reached Purandhar fort foothills; Baji Pasalkar was waiting along with the Maratha army at Purandhar fort. Fateh Khan's army began to advance on the stronghold. Maratha army, under the guidance of Baji Pasalkar, started firing arrows and stones from the top. Baji Pasalkar had strong Maratha warriors like Baji Jedhe, Kavji Malhar, Godaji Jagtap along with him. An intense battle was on. Godaji Jagtap and Muse Khan, second in command of the Fateh Khan army, came face to face, and during the fight, Muse Khan was killed. As soon as Muse Khan fell, his army started fleeing. Fateh Khan, too, started running out of the battleground. Baji Pasalkar, all alone without any military, chased Fateh Khan. While chasing Fateh Khan, Baji Pasalkar came far away from the battlefield. Fateh Khan took advantage of the situation and attacked Baji Pasalkar with his small army force. Baji Pasalkar was surrounded by Fateh Khan's men, and he was killed by them.

This resulted in the death of the first Commander of the Maratha empire. Later Chhatrapati Shivaji Maharaj built a memorial of Baji Pasalkar in Belsar, near Jejuri.

Chapter 6
Sonopant Dabir
"Raajnayik"

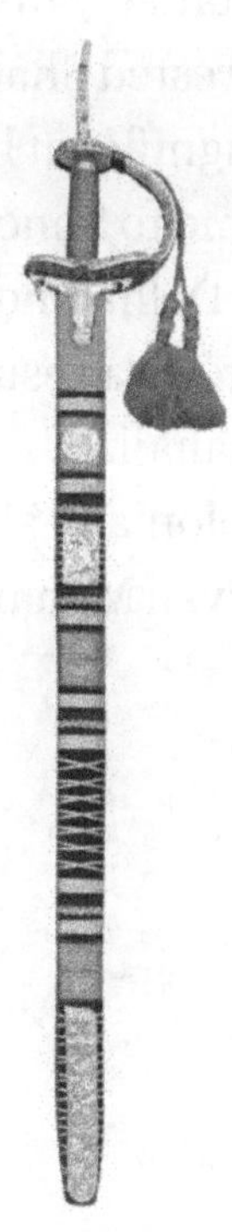

Sonopant Dabir was one of the *Raajnayik* (Diplomat) of Shivaji. He was appointed by Shahaji, father of Shivaji, to assist his son. Sonopant was helping Jijabai and Shivaji with the administrative work of Pune. During the early days of *Swarajya*, he provided crucial guidance to Shivaji.

He was excellent with his diplomatic skills; when Shahaji was arrested by Bijapur Sultanate, his negotiation skills rescued Shahaji. Bijapur Sultanate arrested Shahaji and was planning to kill him. This could have been a significant blow to Shivaji and a dent on *Swarajya*. Responsibility came to Sonopant to ensure safe passage to Shahaji. He traveled to Delhi and discussed the issue with Shahjahan, Mughal Emperor. As a result, diplomatic pressure was put on Adil Shah to release Shahaji.

Sonopant used his diplomatic skills to save Shahji's life and earned more respect from Shivaji Maharaj.

Chapter 7
Murarbaji Deshpande
"Killedar Of Purandhar"

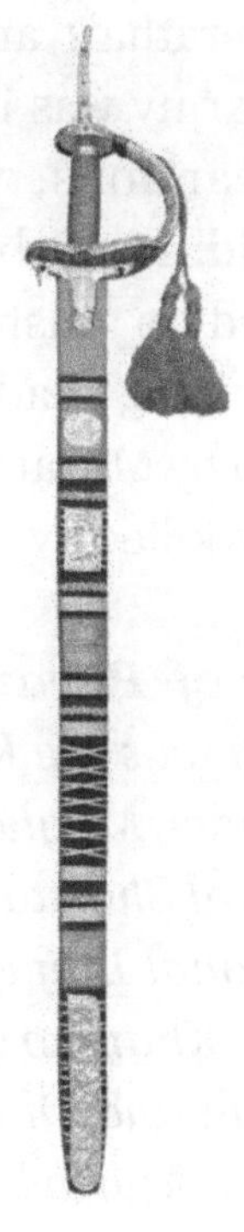

Murarbaji Deshpande was Commander of Maratha Kingdom; initially, he was a part of Chandrarao More's Kingdom in Jawali. He joined the Maratha empire under Shivaji when Shivaji defeated the More Kingdom. Since then, he was a loyal soldier of the Maratha empire under Shivaji and was awarded the title *Killedar* of Purandhar.

In 1665 battle of Purandhar was fought between the Marathas and Mughals. Maratha's army was led by Murarbaji Despande, and the Mughal army was led by Diler Khan. Mughals had superior European cannons, which gave them undue advantages on the battlefield. Murarbaji showed his unmatched swordsman skills and tried to push back Mughals from the Purandhar fort as an inspiring leader. However, despite the extraordinary bravery shown by Murarbaji and his army, Marathas lost this battle. Murarbaji was killed by the Mughal army.

Treaty of Purandhar

Mirza Raja Jai Singh was the King of the Amer Kingdom. The Amer Kingdom was under Mughal control from the time of Akbar. When Mughal General Shaista Khan's attempt to capture Shivaji Maharaj failed, Mughal Emperor Aurangzeb sent Mirza Raja Jai Singh and Diler Khan to capture Shivaji. Seige of Purandhar port by Jai Singh and Diler Khan was a part of this movement. When Shivaji lost Murarbaji and Purandhar fort, he decided to make a truce with Jai Singh. Based on this treaty of Purandhar was signed, and Shivaji surrendered around 23 forts to the Mughals. Later within 3-4 years, all forts were recaptured by Shivaji.

Chapter 8
Netaji Palkar
"Prati Shivaji"

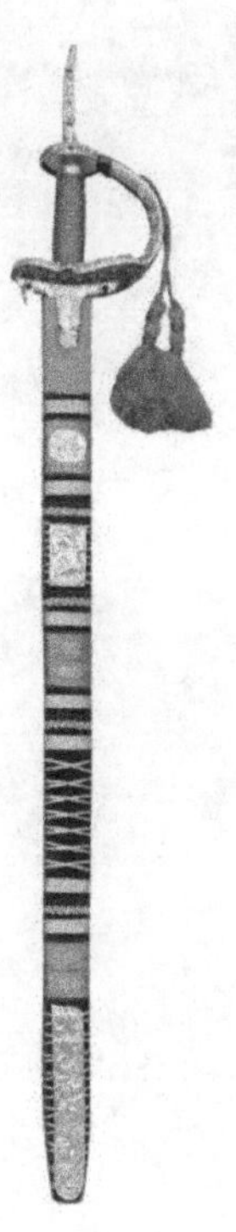

Netaji Palkar was the second Commander in Chief of the Maratha empire under Shivaji Maharaj. In combat, he was a fearsome warrior known as *Prati* Shivaji (Shivaji's Copy). Netaji was part of many successful expeditions and led the Maratha army under his leadership. One of the famous campaigns under him was against Adil Shah of Bijapur after Afzal Khan was killed.

After the treaty of Purandhar, Shivaji surrendered 23 forts to the Mughals, led by Mirza Raja Jai Singh. Post this treaty, Shivaji Maharaj was taken to Agra by Mirza Raja Jai Singh. Shivaji was assured treatment according to royal status by Jai Singh. But when Shivaji was taken to Aurangzeb's royal court, he was made to stand in the third row. Not only that, Aurangzeb didn't even look at Shivaji. This made Shivaji angry and insulted. He walked out of the court to show his displeasure. Later, Shivaji and his son Sambhaji were put under house arrest in a royal guest house by Mughal Emperor.

Meanwhile, Netaji joined the Mughal force under Mirza Raja Jai Singh. On August 17, 1666, Shivaji and his son Sambhaji escaped the royal guesthouse hiding in fruit baskets. Netaji Palkar was captured by the Mughals. They tortured him and forcibly converted him to Islam. Post conversion, his name was changed to Muhammed Kuli Khan. Later he was posted as Mughal Commander in Kandhar fort. He fought many battles for the Mughals. For a decade, he had shown excellent warship skills during his services with Mughals.

Aurangzeb was impressed with the bravery of Netaji, and he was sent to Deccan along with Mughal commander Diler Khan to capture Shivaji's terrain. As soon as he entered Maharashtra, Netaji joined Shivaji and reached Raigad. He was then reconverted to the Hindu religion. Later, Netaji Palkar took charge of the Hujurat division, a personal contingent of Shivaji Maharaj, which always accompanied him in campaigns.

Chapter 9
Moropant Trimbak Pingle
"First Official Peshwa"

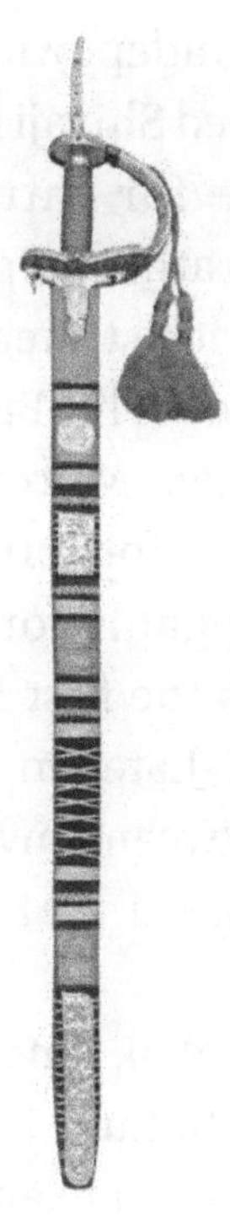

Peshwas were the Prime Ministers of *Chhtrapatis* (Maratha Kings). The word "Peshwa" originated from the Persian language, which meant "foremost." Sonapant Dabir is the first unofficial Peshwa (1640-1652) of Marathas, followed by Shyampant Kulkarni Ranzekar (1652-1657). However, Moropant Trimbak Pingle was officially declared the first Peshwa of the Maratha empire and bore Pant Pratinidhi title. He was a great administrator and was adept with a sword as well. This was a unique combination that helped Shivaji Maharaj to run the empire.

He was responsible for introducing perfect revenue administration for the Maratha empire, helped with resource planning for the army, and made strategies to maintain the strategic forts under Shivaji's kingdom. The Pratapgadh fort holds a vital position in Maratha history; Moropant was responsible for constructing the Pratapgadh fort. In 1657, when most of the construction of the Pratapgadh fort was completed, Shivaji appointed Ganoji Govindji as the first *Killedar* of the fort. By 1659 construction was completed. Later in the same year, the fortress witnessed a historic battle between Shivaji Maharaj and Afzal Khan. Moropant Trimbak Pingle was a part of this Battle and played a strategic role for Marathas.

In 1647 Moropant Trimbak Pingle joined Shivaji to establish the Maratha Empire. Once he became the Peshwa, he participated in many battles fought by Shivaji. For example, he was part of the 1659 Battle against Adil Shah's army post where Shivaji killed Afzal Khan, the General in Adil Shah's Army.

After the death of Shivaji Maharaj, Moropant joined Sambhaji (second Chhatrapati) in many battles for Maratha empire; the battle of Burhanpur was one such Battle.

Moropant Trimbak Pingle died in 1683.

***Peshwa**–In the Maratha Empire, Peshwa was the equivalent of a current-day Prime Minister. Initially, Peshwas were meant to serve Chhatrapati (Maratha King) for administration and defense strategies; however, they later became the decisive leaders for the Maratha empire. Therefore, being Peshwa was pride and came with many responsibilities.*

Chapter 10

Bahirji Naik

"Spy Of Maratha Empire"

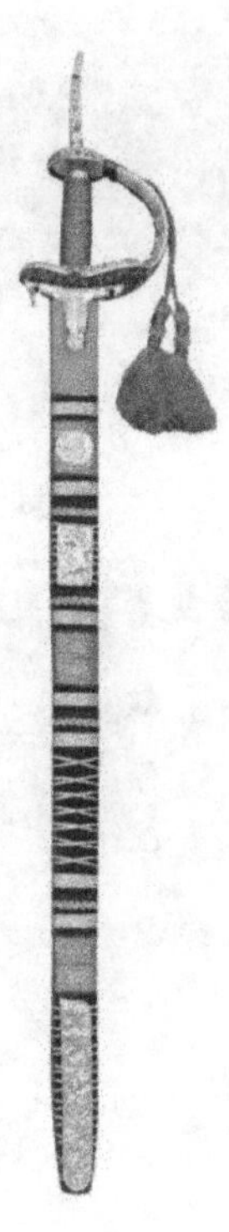

Every successful empire is known for its well-versed army and intelligence team; Shivaji's army was well capable of handling any enemy on the battlefield. Marathas also had a Spy who helped Shivaji Maharaj in many raids and battles. Bahirji Naik, who belonged to the Ramoshi community, was the Spy and efficient soldier of Maratha.

There is a story on how Shivaji has chosen Bhairji Naik as the spy for his *Swarajya* movement. During the early days, Shivaji Maharaj met different Maval communities and provided them with swordfight training to build his army. He used to go inside the jungle and train all Marathas. Shivaji has asked one of his coordinates to sit on the tree during these training sessions. The coordinate's responsibility was to watch the entire Jungle and send out a signal to find someone unknown or a group coming towards training camp. The coordinator used to sit on a tree and closely monitor the movement of all passersby. He sent out a signal by making a peacock sound to alert Shivaji and other Marathas if any unknown person enters the forest. If any unidentified person entered the forest, they would hide their swords and other artillery behind the bush or forest trees. Once the person moves on, they again start practices.

One day Shivaji and others were practicing sword fight. They heard the peacock sound and got alerted. They hid their swords behind the bush and started chit-chatting as if nothing was going on. Everything looked normal there. They saw one guy with a slim body and mustache approaching them. Shivaji was alert. The person came directly towards Shivaji and asked

"What are you all doing here in this jungle?"

To this, Shivaji replied confidently, "We are all friends and came to the jungle for sightseeing."

Guy said with a smile, "Ok, but I have a suggestion; if you don't mind can I tell?"

Surprised, Shivaji replied, "Yes, please go ahead."

The guy replied, “The person who is sitting on the tree to alert you, please ask him not to make Peacock sound during this season. Peacock doesn’t come out during this season and make a sound. The Peacock will not usually make calling noises outside the mating season unless startled between August and February. If your enemy is smart enough, they will know it’s a fake peacock sound and may come to know about your secret plans.”

Shivaji was pleasantly surprised with the intelligence shown by this person; he was none other than Bahirji Naik. So Shivaji decided to make him the Chief Intelligence Officer of his Army.

Over the period, Bahirji’s courage and intelligence induced him to perform espionage in enemy camps. Over many years Marathas used the forefathers of the Ramoshi-Berad community to carry out espionage for raids and intelligence services. His missions and escapades as a spy in Shivaji’s military have made an outstanding contribution to the Maratha empire’s future.

There was one unclaimed incident when Afzal Khan started his journey with his army to capture Shivaji. His war elephant was killed on day 1. It was suspected that Bahirji and his team have poisoned the elephant. This was the act of demoralizing the enemy because a flag-bearing elephant’s death is considered bad luck for any army.

Bahirji Naik was upright at gathering exhaustive information on his missions. Acclaim for many of Shivaji’s astonishing achievements must go to Bahirji Naik and his team. Bahirji had helped Shivaji in many covert operations in enemy terrain. He played a crucial role in many surprise victories and escapes for Shivaji. Bahirji’s tomb is placed in Bhupalgad in Khanapur taluka of Sangli district Maharashtra.

Chapter 11
Samarth Ramdas Swamy
"Spiritual Guru"

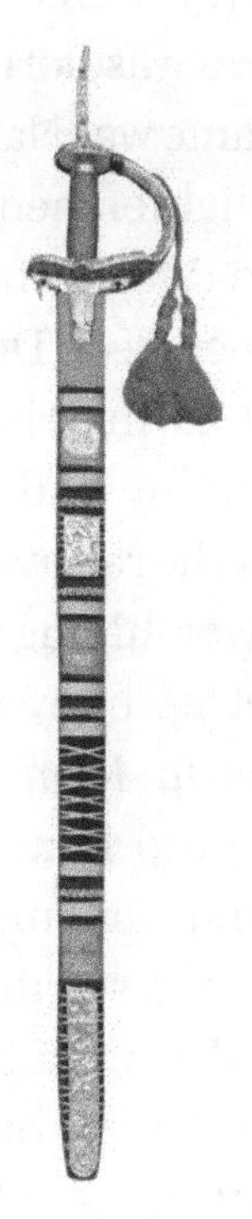

If you have read about Shivaji Maharaj, you would have heard about *Samarth* Ramdas Swamy, the spiritual guru, and well-wisher of Shivaji Maharaj. There are many different views on the relationship between Shivaji and *Samarth* Ramdas Swamy. Some believe Ramdas was the political Guru of Shivaji. On the other hand, some believe that Ramdas was only the spiritual Guru of Shivaji. *Samarth* Ramdas was a follower of Lord Rama and Hanuman. He was born in Jamb Village, located in the Jalana district. His real name was Narayan Suryaji Thosar.

Narayan attained enlightenment at the age of 11 when he heard the adobe voice of Lord Rama, who told him to go to the banks of river Krishna and begin a new sect. During this time, his marriage was fixed; he was reluctant to marriage but agreed to fulfill his mother's wish. However, destiny had something else written for Narayan; on the marriage day, he ran away to Panchvati. For the next 12 years, he spent his time worshiping Lord Ram. During these 12 years, his routine was to get up early morning before sunrise, do yoga, and the carol *"Shri Ram Jai Ram Jai Jai Ram"* till noon. Later in the afternoon, he visited Lord Ram's temple and read spiritual books about Lord Ram. Evening and night were no different, where he used to sing bhajans and read spiritual books before retiring for the day. As he had dedicated his life to Lord Rama, he was later named Ramdas, which means Servant of Ram.

Once Ramdas was sitting near the Godavari river, a set of Brahmins on their way to ashram saw Ramdas, wearing a sadhu's dress but carrying the bow and arrow with him.

Curious brahmins reached out to him, and one of the Brahmins asked, "Hey Child, do you know how to practice this bow and arrow?"

To this, Ramdas replied, "Yes, I do."

Another Brahmin asked, "Can you aim a flying bird on the sky and bring it down?". Ramdas agreed to this request, and within no time, he shot down one bird flying in the high sky with his bow and arrow.

Immediately another brahmin screamed, "Hey Child, what have you done? You have committed a crime by killing an innocent bird."

Ramdas replied, "I did this because you asked me to do so."

Brahmins told Ramdas that he has done wrong by killing an innocent bird and should apologize for the act by performing yagna. Else he would have to face the significances of Karma.

Ramdas agreed to perform the yagna as asked by Brahmins. Once yagna was over, Ramdas asked Brahmins, "As I have now finished yagna to repent my act of killing an innocent bird, am I now free from my sins?". To this, Brahmins confirmed, "Yes, you are."

Ramdas asked, "If I am free from my sin, then why is the bird still dead and not alive?" This question of Ramdas surprised all Brahmins. One of the Brahmins came forward and replied, "No dead bird can come alive."

Ramdas smiled and took the bird in his hand and replied, "If the bird is not alive, then I don't think I am free from my sin" he then took the dead bird closure to his chest and started praying to Lord Ram. Within few seconds bird started breathing, fluttered its wing, and flew away from Ramdas's hand. The full view was a pleasant surprise for all Brahmins standing there and watching an unusual act of Ramdas. Since that day, Ramdas got his new name, *"Samarth Ramdas."*

In 1632 *Samarth* Ramdas left Maharashtra to begin his Spiritual Journey; he travelled throughout the country and observed people's condition in their Motherland. During his spiritual journey, he also met Sikh Guru Hargobind. Once he finished his journey, he decided to spread spirituality amongst people in the country. He also founded a new Sect, *Ramdasi Sampraday*. This sect worshiped Lord Ram, and they also used to practice the battle tactics for their defense. Slowly and steadily popularity of *Samarth* Ramdas spread across Maharashtra and India.

Shivaji was very eager to visit *Samarth* Ramdas Swamy after hearing about his fame. Once they met, Shivaji Maharaj and *Samarth* Ramdas were in regular touch. *Samarth* Ramdas Swamy also wrote a Poem *"Nisaychacha Mahameru"* on Shivaji Maharaj, describing his qualities and character.

Later, on request by Shivaji Maharaj, *Samarth* Ramdas moved to Parali fort near Satara and started living there. The fort was named Sajjangad. It is believed that Shivaji Maharaj also gifted 21 villages to *Samarth* Ramdas and Sajjangad fort.

Samarth Ramdas's contribution to literature is unmatched. A few of his literature is *'Dasbodh,' 'Manache Shlok,' 'Atmaram,' 'Manapanchak,' 'Anandavanbhuvan,'* and much more relevant even in today's world.

Chapter 12
Suryaji Kakade
"Martyr From Battle Of Salher"

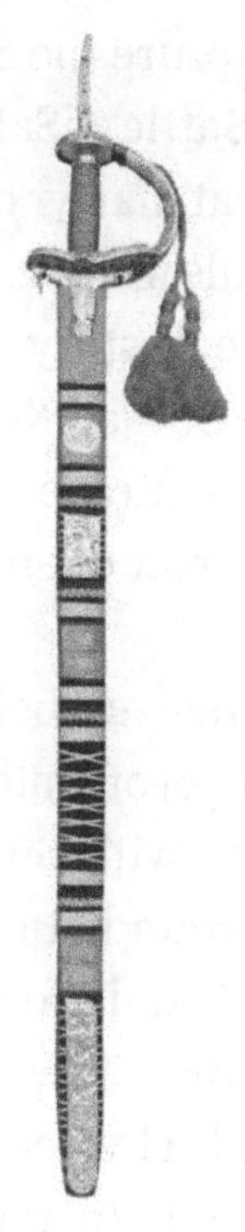

Suryaji Kakade was a childhood friend of Shivaji and joined him from the initial days of the *Swarajya* movement. When Shivaji went to meet Afzal Khan, Suryaji Kakade accompanied him as one of the bodyguards.

In 1671 Shivaji led the army of around 20000 Marathas and captured the Salher fort from Mughals. This was a significant blow to the Mughals, and they wanted to recapture the Salher fort at any cost. The Mughal's attempt to recapture the Salher fort resulted in one of the bloodiest battles, i.e., the Battle of Salher.

Suryaji Kakade is a great martyr of the Battle of Salher, fought between Marathas and Mughals in 1672. This Battle marked a special mention in Maratha empire history. Marathas won this battle against all odds; warriors like Suryaji Kakade, Moropant Pingle, and Prataprao Gujar showed their courage and fought the battle bravely. They ensured that Marathas won open battlefield conflict with the Mughals.

When Mughals and their co-belligerents Rajputs, Pathans, and Rohillas started the siege of Salher, Shivaji sent Moropant Pingle, Prataprao Gujar along with Suryaji Kakade to reclaim the fort. It was estimated that around 10000 soldiers died from both sides in this battle. Suryaji Kakade fought with a brave heart and killed many Mughal armymen. He showed great competence. However, Suryaji Kakade was hit by a cannonball at the last moment, and he died on the battlefield. In the end, Marathas came out victorious in this battle. It was a massive victory for Marathas, though the death of Suryaji Kakde, one of Shivaji's childhood friends, inhibited the Maratha camp's mood.

Such a victory had never been achieved before by Marathas, which ensured that Shivaji Maharaj's fear increased more in Mughal camps. Marathas emerged as a new power to recon in the region. All this was possible due to the sacrifice of great and unknown warriors like Suryaji Kakade.

There is Samadhi of Suryaji Kakade in Salher with moon and sun carved on his Samadhi. This means that his glory will remain on the skyline as long as the moon and sun exist.

Chapter 13
Prataprao Gujar
"When Seven Soldiers Fought Against Seventeen Thousand"

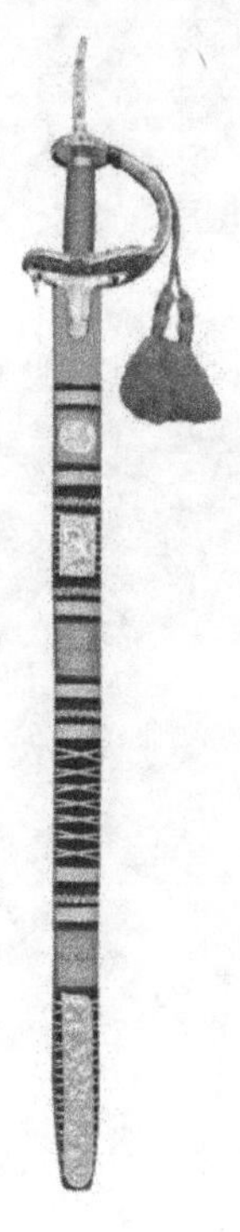

Around April 1673, Prataprao Gujar, the Commander-in-Chief of the Maratha army, was campaigning with his army near Umrani village near Kolhapur. He was responsible for protecting the border with 10000 soldiers from Bahlol Khan of Bijapur, Adlisahi General. Prataprao Gujar defeated the Mughals in a famous battle of Salher, which was significant combat between the Mughals and Marathas. However, even though he was a great warrior, he had one major drawback: his spontaneous emotional nature.

Bahlol Khan was campaigning near a place Nesari. Prataprao Gujar came to know about the location of Bahlol Khan. Without thinking twice, he decided to attack Bahlol's Camp. With his strong army of 10000 soldiers, Prataprao surrounded and blocked out Bhalol Khan. Prataprao's army outnumbered Bhalol Khan's army. Prataprao's strategy was to block the enemy so they won't be able to access water to drink. He ensured the message was clear to Bahlol Khan. If they want to access the water, they have to fight Prataprao's army, waiting for the faceoff with Bahlol Khan's army.

Bahlol Khan knew that if he declares war against Prataprao's army, then indeed, he and his army will get killed within no time. Hence, he didn't want to battle against Prataprao. So, he decided to wait and watch. As it was summer, water scarcity made Bahlol Khan's army life very difficult in the Camp. But they chose to continue in Camp instead of going out for the fight with the Maratha army.

It was a waiting period for both Bahlol Khan and Prataprao, where later was in a commanding position. 3-4 days passed away, and the health condition of Bahlol Khan's army was getting worsened due to a lack of drinking water. Few weeks passed, but the situation didn't change, and many soldiers were on the threshold of getting dead. Bahlol Khan had only two options; either he should surrender to Prataprao OR wait for something to happen from Prataprao's army, which eventually means getting killed by Maratha warrior.

Bahlol Khan finally decided to surrender instead of getting killed. He went to meet Parataprao in his camp for mercy.

"Hey Prataprao, I surrender myself along with my soldiers. So you can take all our horses, weapon, and wealth but please give us water. I promise that we will not come back again here and trouble Marathas" Bhalol Khan was on his knees and begging for a drop of water from Prataprao.

Prataprao was a Hindu. In Hindu culture, giving water to the needy was considered a Nobel onus and the greatest virtue. Bahlol Khan has lost his reputation, and Prataprao was proud enough for this achievement of self and his Maratha army. He gave water to Bahlol Khan and his army and let them go to Bijapur.

Prataprao considered this as his tactical victory and was very satisfied with his achievement. He was eager to share this news with Chhatrapati Shivaji. He wrote a detailed letter to Shivaji, who was staying in the fort of Raigad, about the moral win over Bahlol Khan. He was boasting his strategy and tactics in a letter.

When Shivaji received and read Prataprao's letter, he became agitated and angry at Prataprao. Shivaji was fuming about why the Maratha army could let go of Bahlol Khan alive. They had favorable chances to kill him. He never expected the General of the Maratha army to make such a big mistake; he knew Bahlol Khan is a deceiver and not trustworthy. He will attack Marathas in the next moment if the chance arises. Shivaji knew it's a lost prospect now for Marathas to kill Bahlol Khan.

Shivaji was very upset. He knew the efforts and sacrifices needed to build the Maratha empire. His soldiers' lives are always at stake from enemies. Hence, it was essential to finish the Generals and Leaders of the enemy. In reply to Prataprao's letter, Shivaji wrote a strong reproachful, fuming letter. He asked Prataprao not to show his face to him unless he kills Bahlol Khan. He also wrote that Prataprao should not come to Raigad unless he finishes this task.

When Prataprao read Shivaji's letter, he realized his blunder and never went back to Raigad. He honored Shivaji more than his life; he now wanted to show devotion to his King, who he believed to be the world's supreme King. Moreover, he wanted to do something for the Maratha empire. But Bahlol Khan was currently out of his reach now. He was waiting for a chance to re-encounter Bahlol Khan to kill him and show his loyalty to Shivaji Maharaj.

Prataprao had to wait for almost 10 months for this, on February 24th 1674, when he was on duty to protect the southern border of Maharashtra. He was convoyed by six brave soldiers when they heard that Bahlol Khan campaigned with 17000 of his army nearly half a kilometer away. When Prataprao listened to the name of Bahlol Khan, his face became red with anger. His body was shivering as blood flowed from his toes to his head. Then, without thinking twice, he took out his sword and, on his horse, roared towards the direction of Bahlol Khan's camp.

"Jai Bhavani" Prataprao roared. He wanted to prove something, and the past was bothering him. The remaining 6 soldiers saw their leader marching towards the gorge of death; they had two options: running away or following the leader. They were Marathas, and they were ready to die for the Maratha empire's pride.

"Jai Bhavani" "Har Har Mahadev" all six thundered together, joined Prataprao, and followed him on their horse.

Few *Prehedaar* of Bahlol Khan's Camp saw 7 Marathas are running towards them on their horse with swords in their hand. All 7 Marathas were roaring *"Jai Bhavani" "Har Har Mahadev."* They immediately informed Bahlol Khan; he freaked out when he realized that in those 7 Maratha warriors, Prataprao Gujar is leading the Marathas. He ordered all his 17000 army men to attack 7 soldiers. Bhalol Khan's army also charged towards 7 Maratha warriors.

All 7 Marathas fought bravely against the strong 17000 armies; they knew the result of this fight. They knew they all will die at the end of this battle. Still, they were not fighting this battle to win but to keep the words given to their supreme leader Chhatrapati Shivaji Maharaja. This fight was for their *Raje*. All 7 Maratha warriors were extinct in those 17000 soldiers of Bahlol Khan.

This event shows how commanding respect Shivaji Maharaj had for his soldiers who never feared death. Prataprao and 6 other soldiers knew that they are on an emotional and suicidal mission. None of them will be alive once they have an encounter with 17000 strong armies. But what matters the most for them was respect and devotion towards Shivaji, who has given them the purpose of life and self-respect.

Chapter 14

Senapati Hambirrao Mohite

"Battle Of Wai"

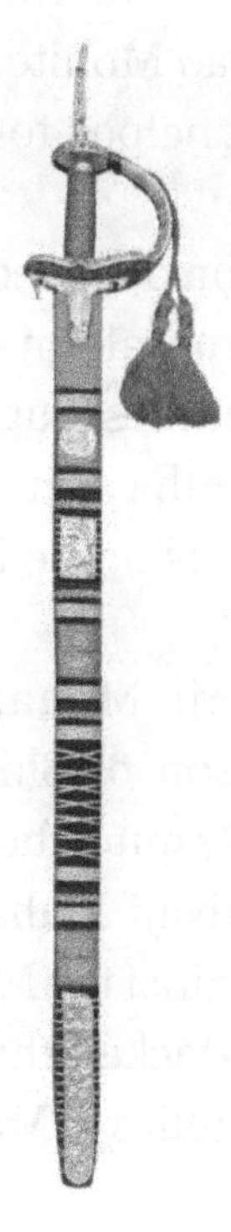

After the death of Prataprao, there was a sense of disbelief in the Maratha camp. They lost one of the greatest warriors, who was the pride of Marathas. Shivaji Maharaj was upset with the event and wanted to replace Prataprao's position with someone as capable as Prataprao. Shivaji wanted to take revenge. He decided to appoint Hansaji Mohite as the next Senapati. Shivaji entitled Mohite as "Hambirrao," and he is popularly known as Hambirrao Mohite since then. He not only met the expectation of Shivaji but helped to push Maratha's pride to the next level.

Hambirrao Mohite soon defeated the Mughal General Bahlol Khan and elevated the lost morale of the Marathas. Later on, he played a crucial role in many battles fought by Shivaji Maharaj.

In 1677 he led the Maratha army to defeat Adil Shahi general Hussain Miyana of Koppal; this battle is famously identified as the "Battle of Koppal."

In 1680 after Shivaji Maharaj's demise, Hambirrao supported Sambhaji (elder son of Shivaji Maharaj) to claim the Maratha throne. This was despite the call of courtiers to crown Rajaram (younger son of Shivaji Maharaj). He also accompanied Sambhaji in his campaigns against the Mughals.

In 1685, Aurangzeb attacked the kingdom of Golkonda and Bijapur. Both kingdoms were allies of Maratha. This dispute resulted in the Battle of Wai.

In December 1687, Hambirrao led the Maratha army in the battle of Wai against the Mughals and defeated a mighty Mughal army. Unfortunately, he got hit by a cannonball during the battle, and he died during the war. Even though Maratha won the war, the loss of Hambirrao cost dearly to Sambhaji's position in the Maratha empire. Hambirrao played a crucial role in keeping many Maratha associates in support of Sambhaji. However, when Hambirrao died during the battle of Wai, many allies deserted themselves from

Sambhaji.

Hambirrao had four sons Santaji, Rangoji, Chandoji, Ranasing, and one Daughter, Tarabai. Daughter of Hambirao, Tarabai was later married to Shivaji's younger son Rajaram and became the Maratha queen.

Chapter 15
Jiva Mahala
"One Who Saved The Life Of Shivaji"

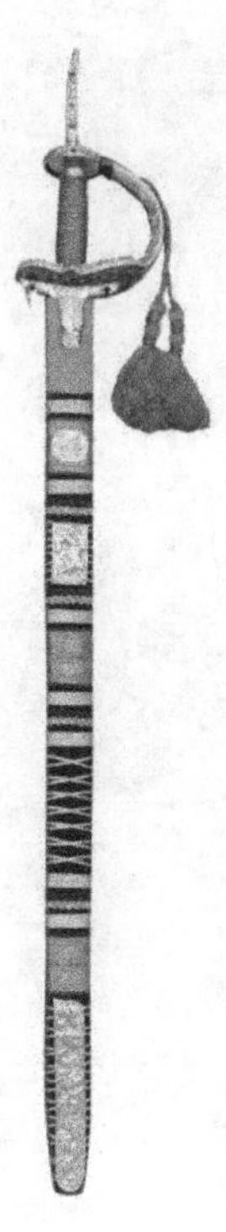

Jiva Mahala was a loyal and trustworthy soldier of Shivaji's army. He was highly skilled in fighting with swords, specially *Danpatta* (Gauntlet-Sword). There is an interesting incident on how Shivaji Maharaj met Jiva.

Once there was one marriage of Maratha soldier in Pune. *Baraat* of marriage was crossing Lal Mahal; this is the palace where Shivaji Maharaj used to stay. In *Baraat,* Shivaji saw one person doing a fantastic entertaining act with Danpatta. Shivaji Maharaj was impressed with the person's sword skills. He was told that the swordsman is Jiva Mahala from a nearby village, and he can hit anything with his sword even at the distance of 10 ft. Shivaji rewarded Jiva for his skills and asked him to join the Maratha army. Jiva instantly agreed; this is how he joined Shivaji's army and became a loyal soldier.

After a few years, when Shivaji Maharaj and Afzal Khan decided to meet at the base of Pratapgadh, it was agreed that both will bring only 10 people from their side for the meeting. Jiva was one among those 10 people chosen by Shivaji to accompany him. He was the personal bodyguard of Shivaji during the meet with Afzal Khan. Therefore, it was Jiva's responsibility to protect Shivaji from any attack during the meeting. Sayyad Banda was the bodyguard of Afzal Khan.

This meeting between Shivaji Maharaj and Afzal Khan went wrong when Afzal Khan tried to kill Shivaji with Khanjar. Shivaji was prepared for such an attack; hence he was wearing shielded armor which protected him from a deadly attack by Afzal Khan. Shivaji swiftly recovered and counterattacked Afzal Khan. Shivaji stabbed Afzal with *baghnakh* and dagger *(Bichwa).*

On hearing the crying voice of Afzal Khan, both Jiva Mahala and Sayyad Banda rushed into the tent where Shivaji and Afzal Khan were there. Sayyad Banda tried to attack Shivaji, however before he could do anything; Jiva Mahala, with his *Danpatta,* chopped off

Sayyad Banda's arm. Shivaji Maharaj, along with his 10 soldiers, escaped the place without getting hurt.

Jiva saved his master's life. Hence, there is a saying in Marathi, *"Hota Jiva Mhanun Vachla Shiva,"* which means if Jiva was not there at that time, Shivaji's life would have been in danger.

Chapter 16
Shiva Kashid
"Chhatrapati Shivaji Of One Day"

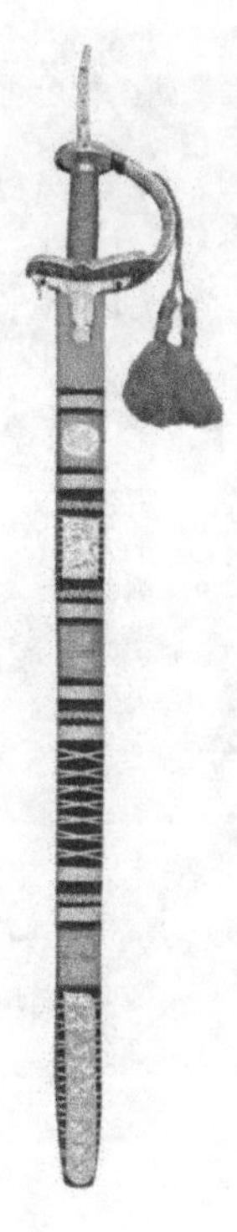

In 1659, Shivaji Maharaj killed Afzal Khan at Pratapghad. Within a short duration, Shivaji also took over Panhala from Ali Adil Shah II, the fifth king of the Adil Shahi sultanate of Bijapur. Post winning Panhala, Shivaji continued spreading his power across the region. This didn't go well with Ali Adil Shah II, and he was preparing to attack Shivaji in Panhala. Siddi Johar, Siddi Masud, and Fazal Khan (son of Afzal Khan) joined this Ali Adil Shah II campaign.

The force of around fifteen thousand men was sent to Panhala fort to win it back from Chhatrapati Shivaji. The siege continued for about 6 months, where all supplies to the fort were cut. It was now becoming difficult for Marathas to survive inside the fortress with essentials. Meanwhile, Fazal Khan attacked Pavangad, the Commander of Pavangad sent an SOS to Panhala for help. Shivaji knew that if Pavangad fell, supplies to Panhala would be cut. This could end up Marathas in the Panhala fort starving and dying. Moreover, Shivaji knew he may get captured any moment by Ali Adil Shah's Army. The only option left with Maratha was that Shivaji should escape from Panhala without the enemy's knowledge.

Shivaji's main confidants in this escape plan were his commander-in-chief Baji Prabhu Deshpande, Chief of Intelligence Bahirji Naik, and his barber Shiva Kashid. A detailed plan was prepared where the hidden route was decided through some thick forests, which will be used by Shivaji to escape. Representatives from the Maratha army were sent to General Siddi Johar, asking for a meeting between him and Shivaji's emissary for a mutual agreement. Siddi Johar agreed to the forum, and the meeting date was decided. In a planned way, a day was chosen when heavy rain was expected due to monsoon; this would have helped Shivaji escape. Maratha planned to distract the enemy with talks of the meeting. Shivaji would escape via hidden routes from forests in heavy rain.

On the evening of the meeting, Siddi Johar's soldiers spotted one palanquin with a small troupe of Maratha soldiers trying to escape from the fort. The alarm was raised, and Maratha soldiers and Shivaji in Palanquin were captured and brought to Siddi Johar. The entire captured troupe of prisoners, including Shivaji, were paraded for verification, as Siddi Johar has never seen Shivaji. He wanted to be sure that his army has captured Maratha King and not anyone else. All Maratha prisoners confirmed that the person arrested by Johar's army is indeed Great Chhatrapati Shivaji.

During this verification process, news came that a different palanquin, escorted by around 600 Maratha soldiers, has made its way to Vishalgad. So, the real Shivaji was escaped to Vishalgad, and the first palanquin had Shivaji's dupe, Shiva Kashid.

Siddi understood that the person caught is not Shivaji but a dupe. So then, in a fit of anger, Siddi Johar beheaded Shiva Kashid.

Shiva Kashid, the brave man who sacrificed his life for Shivaji, was the personal barber of Shivaji. Kashid was an exact look-alike as Shivaji and bore a resemblance to the Chhatrapati Shivaji. This unique feature of Kashid was noticed by Commander-in-chief Baji Prabhu Deshpande. So, he planned to distract the enemy with a body double and make way for Shivaji's escape. However, Shivaji was reluctant about this as he knew it will risk the life of Kashid. But respect and importance of Shivaji in every Maratha's life were superior to their individual lives. So, Shiva Kashid agreed to a suicidal mission and dressed up like Chhatrapati Shivaji and deceived the enemies to save Shivaji's life. This way, he became Chhatrapati Shivaji for One Day.

Chapter 17
Baji Prabhu Deshpande
"Battle Of Pavan Khind"

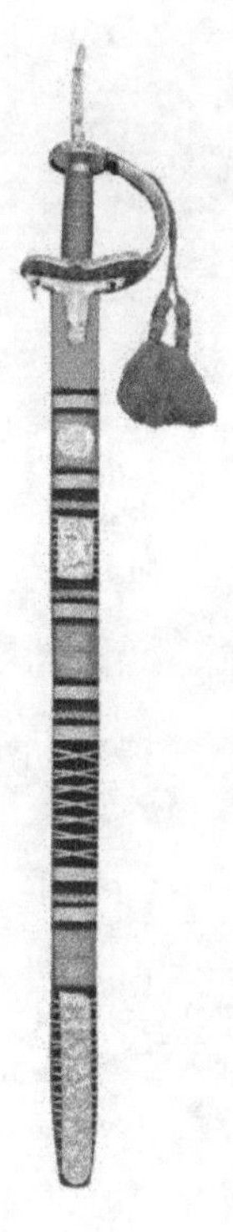

Baji Prabhu Deshpande was a General in the Maratha army. Like Shiva Kashid, he too sacrificed his life to save Chhatrapati Shivaji Maharaj. He was one of the Commander in chief with Shivaji at Panhala against the siege by Siddi Johar. During the siege, when it became evident that Shivaji must escape Panhala, Baji Prabhu executed an escape plan for Shivaji and the Maratha army. He prepared an intent to use Shiva Kashid as Shivaji Maharaj and deceive Siddi Johar. In parallel with around 600 trusted soldiers, Baji Prabhu led Chhatrapati Shivaji out of Panhala on a rainy night.

As per plan on a stormy night, around 600 soldiers led by Shivaji and Baji Prabhu will take a secret route through a thick forest to come out of Panhala. Another small troop will be sent out with Shiva Kashid (look-alike of Shivaji) to deceive Siddi Johar's Army. When the plan of deceiving Siddi Johar by Shiva Kashid was busted, Siddi Johar killed Shiva Kashid. Johar's soldiers were now aware of escape plans despite Baji Prabhu's best attempts to ensure a safe getaway to Shivaji. Shiva Kashid's heroic martyrdom did help to get more time for Shivaji's troops to reach Vishalgadh securely.

Siddi Johar sent out a massive number of the army to chase down Shivaji Maharaj. The Maratha warriors gashed through the rainy night on their horses. Finally, they reached Pavan Khind (earlier known as Ghod Khind), a narrow mountain area that could let only 3-4 people from the slender passage. All Marathas and Shivaji Maharaj were standing at the starting point. They all knew that Johar's army is not far behind them and will reach there at any time. All 600 Marathas couldn't cross the narrow lane before Johar's army reaches there. They were well aware that Johar's army will outnumber them. Without much thought, Baji Prabhu volunteered himself and around 300 Marathas decided to face Johar's army at the pass; so that Shivaji and the remaining Maratha soldiers could proceed to Vishalgad fort. Shivaji didn't agree to this and was reluctant to leave his soldiers for an apparent death. But Baji Prabhu, along with other Marathas, requested and convinced Shivaji to proceed to Vishalgad. For Marathas more than their life, what matters was Shivaji and *Hindavi Swarajya.* With a heavy heart, Shivaji agreed to move along with the remaining 300 odd Maratha soldiers. It was decided that once Shivaji reaches the destination safely, three cannon bullets will be fired to send out the signal to Baji Prabhu.

Once Shivaji moved out, Johar's Army reached the passage where Baji Prabhu waited with his Maratha army. Marathas were massively outnumbered; as per some historians, Maratha and Johar's Army ratio was 1:100 ratio, and some say it was a 1:40 ratio. Whatever be the number ratios, but Maratha fought this battle fabulously. Johar's Army was ruthless, and they kept attacking Marathas. The latter blocked the narrow passage and made it difficult for Johar's Army to cross the route. Slowly and steadily, Marathas were losing their soldiers. However, Baji Prabhu was standing like a strong wall and was giving a tough fight. He carried two heavy swords in his hands and used his body as a wall; he prevented anyone from going through the passage. He got severely injured during the fight but didn't give up and kept fighting to ensure no one from Johar's army went through the passage. He was determined not to quit until he hears the cannon shots, ensuring that Shivaji is safe.

Even though Shivaji moved on from the narrow passage of Pavan Khind, he had to defeat Mughal Sardar Surve to reach the Vishalgad fort. Shivaji attacked Surve's army with his Maratha soldiers and captured the Vishalgad fort. As planned, once the fort was captured, cannon shots boomed from the distant Vishalgad to send out a signal to Baji Prabhu that Shivaji is safe, and he captured the Vishalgad. It was almost dawn and almost 5-6 hours since the battle on Pavan Khind started. Baji Prabhu was still on his legs, badly wounded but with the same spirit at the beginning of the fight. He and his soldiers have been given a tough fight and were successful in saving their King. When Baji Prabhu heard the cannon shot boom, he was relieved, and with a massive call of *"Jai Bhavani"* Baji Prabhu passed away with a smile on his face, with both swords still in his hand. During the Battle, only a few Marathas survived, but their enemies' casualties numbered in thousands. Finally, Maratha soldiers cleared the pass and carried the body of Baji Prabhu to Vishalgad.

Shivaji was heartbroken when he came to know about the death of Baji Prabhu. Shivaji renamed gorge narrow pass from Govind Khind to Pavan Khind and offered "honor of court" to Baji Prabhu's family.

Chapter 18

Firangoji Narsala

"Fighter Killedar"

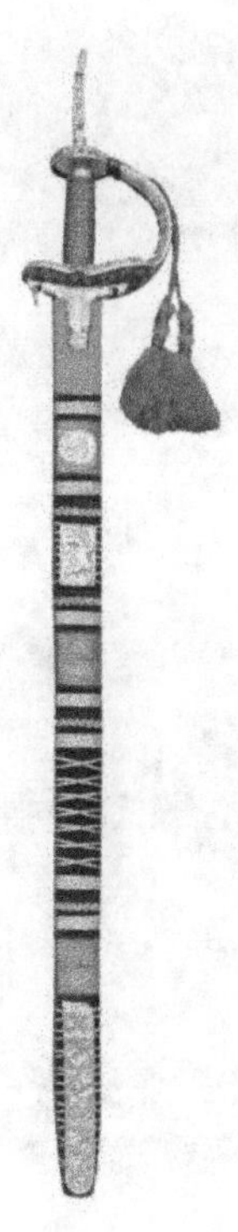

Firangoji Narasala was one of the trusted Maratha commanders of Shivaji Maharaj. During the 17th Century, he was *Killedar* (commander of the fort) of Sangram Durg fort in Chakan. During this time, Shaista Khan, the General in the Mughal Army, planned to invade Pune and capture the Maratha empire. He planned to mobilize around 1 lakh soldiers for this campaign. Attack was planned strategically. Shaista Khan decided to attack Sangram Durg fort first and capture it from Marathas.

So Shaista's campaign began in June 1660 with around 20000 soldiers where he attacked Sangram Durg fort. Fort was protected by *Killedar* Firangoji Narasala, who was accompanied by only 320 odd soldiers. Indeed, Marathas were outnumbered compared to the Mughal Army. Firangoji was aware of Mughal's plan. He was prepared for the long battle to protect the Sangram Durg fort. Shivaji Maharaj knew that Marathas will lose the Sangram Durg fort. He didn't want the casualties of his soldiers deployed there. Hence before Shaista's attack on Sangram Durg, Shivaji sent a message to Firangoji Narasala and asked him to leave the fort with Maratha soldiers. However, a fighter in Firangoji didn't allow him to go out of the fort, and he was determined to fight with the Mughals.

Firangoji decided not to leave the fort and, with the help of limited soldiers, defended the fort for 56 days. During these 56 days, the Mughals tried very hard to capture the fort; however, Maratha's guerrilla war techniques made their lives difficult.

As the fight got more challenging, Shaista decided to take a different approach to defeat Firangoji's army. Mughals dug a tunnel up to the fort, and it was filled with explosives. When blast was executed on this tunnel, it blew up the wall of the Sangram Durg fort. Almost 75 Maratha soldiers died in this attack. This was a significant blow to Marathas.

Mughal army marched into the fort, and final fighting resulted in the death of more Marathas soldiers as they were outnumbered. Even after the outer wall of the fort was ruptured by heavy cannons, the Marathas kept fighting. Eventually, the fort was captured by Shaista Khan. Still, he was overwhelmed by the way Firangoji made the Mughals struggle to capture the fort. He was very much impressed by the bravery of Firangoji Narasala. He offered him a respectful post in the Mughal Army. However, Firangoji was a true Maratha and loyalist of Shivaji Maharaj; he declined the offer of Shaista Khan. Later Shaista provided the safe passage to Firangoji and the remaining Maratha soldiers to move out of Sangram Durg fort.

Firangoji returned with his soldiers and met Shivaji Maharaj. He was feeling guilty for not being able to protect the fort from Shaista Khan's Army. He apologized to Shivaji. However, on contradict, Shivaji Maharaj was pleased with the way Firangoji and a small troupe of Maratha soldiers defended a small fort-like Sangram Durg for almost 2 months without any support from outside. Even though they were outnumbered by the Mughals, it took 2 months to capture the fort. Shivaji was thrilled the way Firangoji led Marathas has given a tough fight to Mughals. He was now sure that he has brave soldiers in hand, and he can defeat any enemies of the Maratha kingdom any day.

Chapter 19
Kondaji Farzand
"Recapturing Panhala Fort"

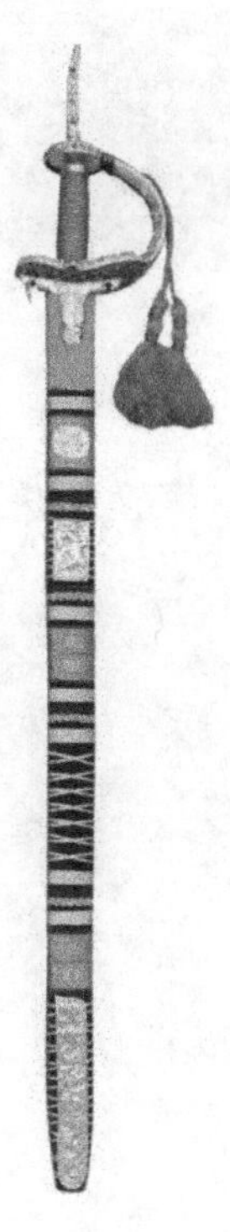

Panhala fort is located strategically overlooking the Sahyadri mountain range near Kolhapur. During the Adil Shahi regime, this was a critical trade route from Bijapur to the region's coastal areas. Therefore, having control of the Panhala fort was necessary, considering transport routes for successful trades. As this was a crucial route, having control of the Panhala fort was very important for rulers. Due to this, Panhala fort has seen many battles involving Mughals, Marathas, and Britishers.

Under Adil Shahi's rule of Bijapur, the Panhala fort was built with solid walls and entrances around the fort to ensure that it becomes impossible to concur. Shivaji Maharaj wanted the Panhala fort in Maratha control. With this intention, during 1660, he attacked the Panhala fort with his army. However, this attempt to capture the Panhala fort by Shivaji failed, and he lost many of his men. This defeat didn't go well with Shivaji. He wanted to capture the Panhala fort at any cost. He waited for the right time, and after 13 years, he decided to plan an attack again in Panhala fort. This time Kondaji Farzand, one of the Maratha warriors, volunteered to lead this ambitious attack of Shivaji Maharaj. During that time, the Panhala fort was defended by the strong 1500+ soldiers of Adil Shah. Surprisingly, as an attack strategy, Kondaji Farzand decided to take only around 300 army men.

Kondaji Farzand knew that he could not go full out for an open attack to capture the fort. Hence he decided to camp near Panhala fort for around 2 months to gather detailed information of enemies like how many shifts are done to protect the regiment, how many soldiers are deployed per shift, where the strongest fortresses are, how the entire process of surveillance is done. After 2 months, Marathas got crucial information that the south of the fort has minimum surveillance based on all information. This side had a straight valley down with a thick, dense forest. So Kondaji Farzand decided to take this route to attack the fort. He decided to take only

60 men along with him in the mission, and the remaining Maratha army was kept at the base of the fort. This was to ensure that if enemy soldiers run towards the forest for escape or take any help, Marathas waiting in the bottom of the fort, will do a counterattack. This will block the enemies completely.

On the night of the attack, 60 Marathas led by Kondaji climbed the fort wall, entered the fort, and attacked the Adil Shahi's soldiers. They were shocked by the surprise attack. Marathas, who were at the fort base, started making loud sounds with bugle and clarion; already shocked enemies panicked by hearing these loud noises from the fort base. They thought a large army of Martaha have outnumbered them and will kill all of them in no time. As planned, Adil Shahi's soldiers panicked and started running leaving behind the fort. Marathas attacked in full force and captured the Panhala fort. Kondaji Farzand played a critical role in getting the Panhala fort back to Shivaji Maharaj.

Chapter 20
Lal Mahal
"Recapturing Pune"

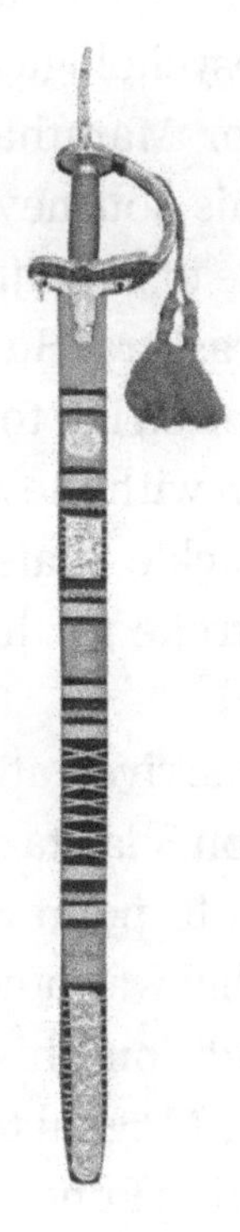

One of the critical events in the early 1660s was Shaista Khan's attack on Pune and siege in Shivaji's residence, Lal Mahal. Later, with his small but powerful battalion, Shivaji breached and shooed away an embarrassed Shaista Khan to Bengal.

Once Aurangzeb became the Mughal Emperor, he sent Shaista Khan with around one lakh soldiers to capture Pune. Having control of Pune would give a psychological advantage to Mughals and will be a substantial blow for Marathas. Pune was important for Shivaji as he has started his journey of *Swarajya* from Pune. Aurangzeb knew the total size of Shivaji's army is meaningfully less and is scattered across Maharashtra. He wanted to capture the entire Deccan province in one major strike to Marathas. Shivaji knew he could not defeat Shaista Khan with the Army in a direct ground war and needed to strategically tackle Shaista Khan. He knew guerrilla warfare will be the masterstroke for him and Marathas to defeat Shaista Khan.

In 1660 Shaista Khan arrived at Aurangabad with the Army and moved towards Pune. Soon Shaista captured Pune and set up his camp in Lal Mahal; this was to point Shivaji that Pune no longer belongs to Marathas. Lal Mahal was built by Shahaji Bhosale, in the 1930s for his wife Jijabai and Son Shivaji. Shaista took control of Pune and started ruling as per Mughal terms and conditions. All the locals were banned from entering Pune.

As time passed on, Shivaji planned to attack Shaista Khan. On April 5, 1663, Shivaji and his closed armymen disguised as the bridegroom's procession members entered Pune. This was a trap created by Shivaji for the Mughal army. Shaista Khan and his Army were not prepared for such a surprise attack. Shivaji was aware of all passages and gates of the palace very well. Within no time, as soon as Shivaji and his men entered the court, they started attacking and killing Shaista's army. Shivaji entered the sleeping chamber of Lal

Mahal, where Shaista was sleeping. Shaista realized the danger and ran towards the chamber window and jumped out of the window. However, before he could escape, Shivaji swung his sword towards Shaista to kill him. Still, Shaista was lucky enough to miss the deadly sword swing of Shivaji, but the sword struck his hand, chopping away Khan's three fingers. By this time, the entire Mughal army was alarmed by the gurriella attack by Shivaji and his army. That day Shivaji not only chopped Shaista Khan's finger but also chopped Mughal's pride.

Shivaji and his men left the scene and escaped to Sinhagad. This attack immensely increased the Shivaji as a great warrior in the region. Moreover, on the other hand, it caused a momentous humiliation for the Mughals. This was a masterstroke by Shivaji to ruin all the status Mughals gained from 1660 till 1663. As a consequence of this attack, Shaista Khan was moved to Burhanpur and later shifted to Bengal.

Very soon, Shivaji recaptured Pune from the Mughals and regained Maratha's pride.

Chapter 21
Era Of Chhatrapati Shivaji
(1674 -1680)

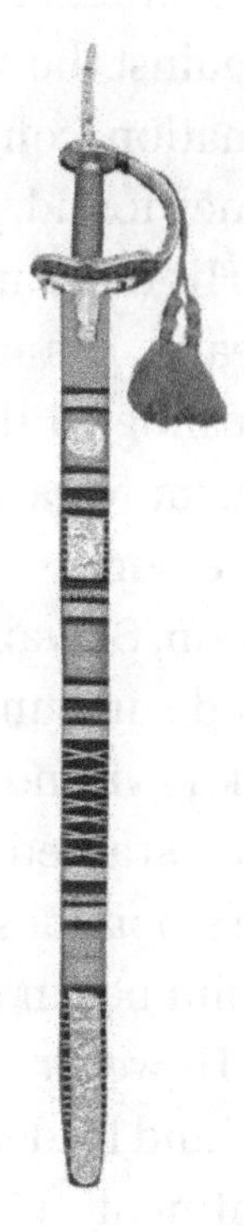

On the fateful day of June 6, 1674, Shivaji was conferred upon the titles of Chhatrapati (one who is the paramount sovereign), *Haindava Dharmodhaarak* (the savior of the Hindu religion), and *Shakakarta* (the founder of a new era). He enthrones himself, thereby challenging the authority of the Mughals by contradicting the custom of seeking permission in the Mughal-dominated India. Thereby marking the official mutiny against the Mughals, the downfall of the Mughal Empire, and the formation, congregation, and escalation of the Maratha empire. With newfound purpose and vigor, Shivaji marched towards the South. His determination was more vital than ever despite his weakening health. His aggressive campaign tactfully included diplomatically appealing to the people of the south and awakening a sense of patriotism towards their land and repulsion against the outsiders and oppressors.

By the time of coronation, Shivaji already etched his name in the history of the Maratha and surrounding regions. His valor and aggressive battle tactics were known and feared far and wide.

As Maratha's efforts started streamlining under the leadership of Shivaji, people's opinions and those of well-wishing rulers and warriors around him began to strengthen regarding the need for an official kingship. However, the road to becoming a king from an undefeatable warrior and leader wasn't an easy one. Shivaji faced opposition and resentment from more spaces than one. Neither did his views align with fellow warriors politically on the same footing as his, nor did his lineage justify the kingship according to the stringent caste system followed in the Hindu society.

However, no backing or resistance of any of the forces could swerve Shivaji's resolution to pursue and lead the Maratha empire to absolute freedom. Shivaji surpassed the barrier that no one could ever imagine with his tenacious negotiation skills and inventive planning. He was initiated with the life of the twice-born. He went on to take up not one title but three, which practically changed the history we know today and the future of the then Maratha empire.

In his conquest of the South, he captured politically important military bases like the Bijapur, Ponda, Karwar, Kolhapur, and forts of Vellore and Gingee. With Golkonda's Qutub Shah on his side, Shivaji's consolidation in Karnataka became more effortless than the tight rope walk it was supposed to be. Shivaji had an unbeatable sense of tactic; he knew when to use diplomacy and when to straight out go to war. His conflict with his half-brother Venkoji was exemplary in this sense as Shivaji resorted to battling him out after several failed attempts at negotiations. The result was Shivaji's stranglehold in another base of economic and political importance, the Mysore Plateau.

As the Maratha flag was hoisted in several southern regions, a contending power, the Kingdom of Mysore resisted against the Marathas and thus began a power struggle.

Chapter 22

Yesaji Kank

"Warrior Who Crushed Elephant"

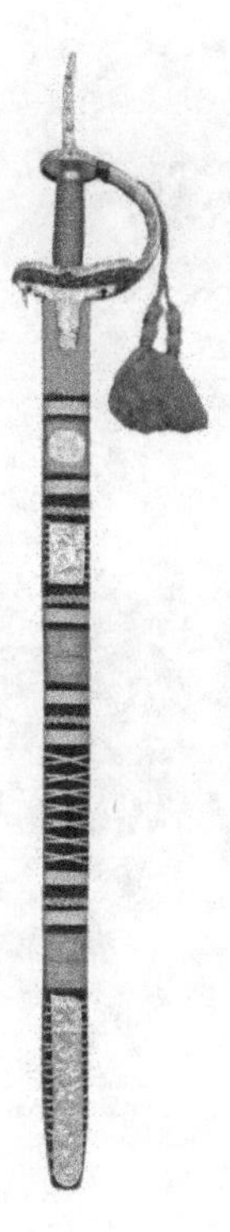

In 1677, Shivaji Maharaj was scheduled to attack Adil Shah during his most extended campaign to the south of India. For that, an alliance with Qutub Shah of Golkonda was vital. Shivaji Maharaj visited Qutub Shah after his coronation before his military campaign in the South. When Qutub Shah came to know about the interest of Shivaji for an alliance, he showed his willingness to welcome Shivaji and his envoy in his capital. On arriving at the palace of Qutub Shah, Shivaji received a warm welcome. Shivaji stayed there for almost a month and formally concluded the historic alliance with Golkonda State.

During his stay, many cultural and war displays happened between Shivaji and Qutub Shah's army. For example, Golkonda's army had giant elephants, which were desirable for Qutub Shah during wars. But, on the contrary, there were no elephants in the Maratha army; they mainly trusted in their fast and quick Maratha soldiers. Qutub Shah was stunned to see no single elephant in Shivaji's army and despite that Maratha has won many battles.

Curious, Qutub Shah asked Shivaji, "Maharaj, I wonder why you don't have elephants in your army?"

Marathas used guerilla warfare techniques that needed fast execution. Using elephants in such warfare would drop the speed of the entire mission. Moreover, Marathas mainly fought on forts or on hilly areas where heavy animals like elephants were not intelligent to use. But instead of providing details to Qutub Shah, Shivaji smiled and responded, "I don't need an elephant in my army as each Maratha warrior is equivalent to the elephant."

By now, Qutub Shah and Shivaji had become good friends, so taking the liberty of this Qutub continued

"So, let's have competition between my elephant and your elephant," and he laughed.

"Sure, why not?" Shivaji replied instantly and looked at his Maratha warriors sitting a few meters away from him and hearing the conversation between two Kings.

Within no time, one warrior came out of the Maratha army who was tall and had an athletic personality. He had a sword in his hand and stood on open ground where one elephant from Qutub Shah's army was already there. The Maratha warrior was Yesaji Kank. The fight was about to start where one side was a gigantic elephant; on another side, there was a trusted Maratha warrior of Shivaji, Yesaji Kank.

There was no fear in the eyes of Yesaji. The elephant started moving towards him. As soon as the elephant was feet away from Yesaji, he dodged the elephant, jumped on the right side of the elephant, and slit the elephant's leg with his sword. Blood started floating from the elephant's leg. The elephant was furious; he wanted to crush the person who injured him. Yesaji was alert and was observing every movement of an elephant. But this time elephant moved quicker and captured Yesaji with his trunk. Everyone on the ground was still and was in shock. The view was bloodcurdling; any moment, the elephant will smash Yesaji on the ground and kill the great Maratha warrior.

It was an elephant's turn to take vengeance. The elephant threw Yesaji into the air; the Maratha army closed their eyes and could not see Yesaji getting killed brutally. But before anyone could open their eyes, they heard a loud trumpet crying sound. When they opened their eyes, they all witnessed an incredible view. When the elephant threw Yesaji into the air, he swings his sword like a rumble of thunder and cuts the elephant's trunk into two pieces. The elephant was on its knees and was crying in pain. Yesaji was standing in front of the elephant with a sword bathed with blood.

Shivaji stood up proudly and proclaimed to all that Sardar Yesaji Kank is his elephant. Qutub Shah was is in shock to see the unbelievable act of human defeating the giant animal. This never happened in the history of Qutub Shahi. He offered gifts to Yesaji for his brave deed; however, Yesaji politely refused the same.

Yesaji Kank was head of the Maratha army. He was a brave general and loyal to Chhatrapati Shivaji till the death of Shivaji. Yesaji Kank was from the small village Bhutonde near Rajgad. He was one of the oldest aides of Shivaji who perceived Shivaji's 35-year war against Mughal and Adil Shahi. He was one of the utmost dependable men of Shivaji Maharaj.

Chapter 23
Series Of Defeat and Death Of Chhatrapati Shivaji Maharaj

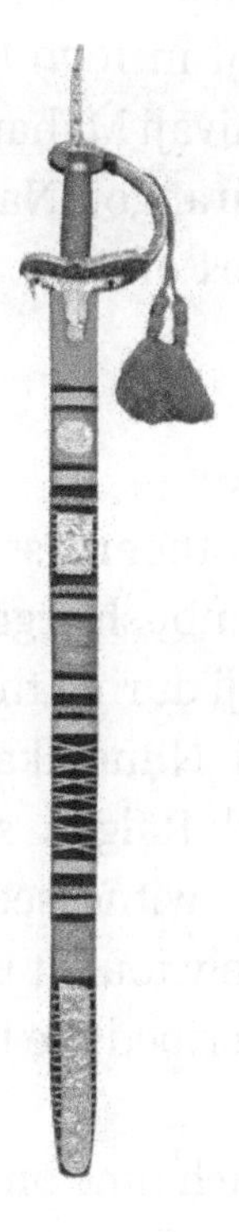

Several battles were fought after Shivaji Maharaj assumed his position as the Chhatrapati. However, things started to look difficult during this period for the Maratha empire. A series of lost battles and losing many warriors caused immense loss of life and territories.

Battle of Bhupalgadh

This battle was fought in 1679 between the Mughal viceroy Diler Khan and Marathas. Shivaji Maharaj was at the forefront along with notable warriors like Firangoji Narsala and his son Sambhaji. The battle ended with the fort of Bhupalgadh being demolished by the Mughal forces.

Battle of Sangamner

The same year saw another massive defeat of the Marathas. It manifested as a result of an ambush organized to trap and kill Shivaji Maharaj. The safety of Shivaji during the war was guaranteed by his loyal warriors like Siddhoji Nimbalkar. He sacrificed his life to ensure that Shivaji reached Raigad safely to carry forward the Maratha legacy. This war also witnessed the notable contribution of Santaji Ghorpade, who bravely fought until Shivaji was routed. The battlefield of Sangamner inscribed the last ever footprints of Shivaji Maharaj's on a battlefield.

Shivaji did not get much time on the throne. A few years after his coronation, he fell seriously sick, and his eldest son's unjust rebellion was doing no good to him. Sambhaji's reckless war tactics and aggression combined with his lack of responsibility and repentance made Shivaji reconsider if he was the suitable successor to the throne. Unfortunately, Shivaji didn't have enough time to announce a decision before he succumbed to dysentery in the early days of April 1680.

The entire country grieved the loss of the undeniably greatest emperor and warrior that India had seen up to that date. He was revered by even his sworn enemies. Arguably some historian says that even Aurangzeb paid tribute to Shivaji post his death. He noted that Shivaji was a great warrior who dared to raise an independent Kingdom, fought with Mughals for almost 2 decades, and kept increasing his territories.

Shivaji owned unparalleled courage, guerrilla warfare tactics, diplomatic dexterity, and undying patriotism. He left behind an inspirational motive to the coming generations of Maratha warriors and a legacy worshiped today.

However, internal politics worsened within his family, with Sambhaji's ambition being on a higher pedestal than his relations. As the eldest son, he was technically entitled to the throne without any deserving candidates. However, Shivaji's second wife, Soyarabai, with the help of Shivaji's close ministers, crowned her 10 years old son Rajaram on the throne. As a result, Sambhaji revolted in full force and took over the kingdom and the Raigad fort. Effectually imprisoning his step-brother and step-mother, who was later decapitated, allegedly on manufactured conspiracy charges against the Chhatrapati.

Chattrapati Succession Tree

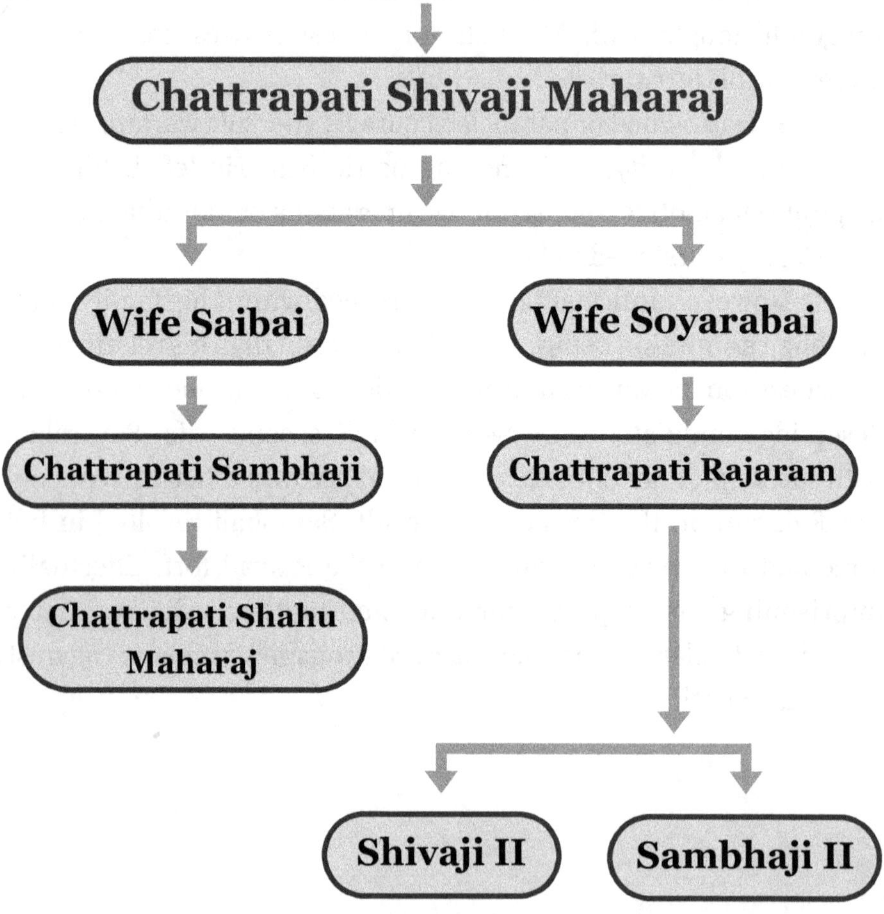

Chapter 24
Sambhaji Maharaj
"Dharamveer Of Hindavi Swarajya"

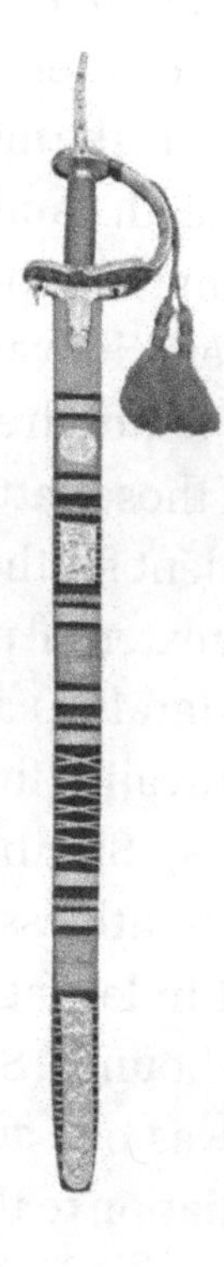

Sambhaji, the eldest son of Shivaji Maharaj, was born on 14th May 1657 at fort Purandhar. People fondly address Sambhaji as Shambu Raje. But, unfortunately, his life was short-lived, and his death was catastrophic. His death shook the entire Marathas, and it was the beginning of a fresh rise of *Hindavi Swarajya*. Even today, he is consecrated as a true Hindu Martyr as he preferred a death against a dishonorable life. Sambhaji's mother, Saibai, died when he was very young. He was raised by his grandmother Jijabai, the mother of Shivaji Maharaj.

Post Shivaji Majaraj's death Sambhaji was crowned as second Chhatrapati of the Maratha Empire. From an early age, he was a well-versed scholar and was fluent in various languages. Sambhaji Maharaj fought more than a hundred battles, and as per few historians, he never lost any of those battles.

Shivaji had set a precedent for the Maratha warriors to follow against the Mughals and other external powers by embedding feeling of Deccan patriotism in the Marathas and down south. But, rather contrastingly, more than Shivaji's first preferred strategic and diplomatic planning tactics, Sambhaji tried to control the neighboring territories through ruthlessness and coercion.

While Shivaji believed in letting war captives peacefully go, Sambhaji's atrocities knew no bounds. Sambhaji's barbaric attack on the Burhanpur fort in 1680 was one such example. However, it is believed to be justified in retaliation to the extreme nature of outrage Mughal in charge shown in the region. As a result, Sambhaji's forces went on a deadly offensive. They routed the Mughals to the extent of setting the city's ports ablaze.

Famous Campaigns Against Mughals

There were many famous campaigns lead by Sambhaji, which resulted in enormous benefits for the Maratha Empire. In 1680 he challenged Mughal monarch Bahadur Khan Koka. His first crusades were against Burhanpur, which was a stronghold of the Mughals then. Burhanpur is currently in Madhya Pradesh. Bahadur Khan was in charge of Burhanpur; this place was known for its treasures and grand structures. Sambhaji knew if Marathas capture Burhanpur, it will be a big moral victory for Marathas and a significant blow to Mughal's reputation. Marathas, under the command of Hambirrao Mohite, attacked Burhanpur and captured the city. They were able to loot all of Mughal's treasury and animals. Corresponding to the attack on Burhanpur, Sambhaji strategized to attack the Mughals on three fronts. Three platoons of Maratha warriors were made; one platoon attacked the Mughal territory of Surat. The second platoon raided Khandesh, and the third one took on Mughals in Aurangabad. All these attacks were successful, and Maratha emerged as the winner. They captured a good amount of wealth and ammunition from the Mughals.

The uprising of Sambhaji Maharaj for 8 years made Aurangzeb vow that he won't wear his crown until he arrests Sambhaji Maharaj.

Attack On Mysore

Chikka Devaraja was the founder ruler of Mysore who encroached into specific Maratha territory. When Sambhaji learned about this, he sent his ambassador to Mysore. But his ambassador was not treated well in Mysore court. This made Sambhaji furious, and he decided to attack Chikka Devaraja. Under the leadership of Sambhaji, Maratha army marched towards Mysore; however, Chikka Devaraja's army was well prepared for any battle. Devaraja's army stopped Marathas outside Mysore territory. Maratha's army was greeted by the Mysore army with a hefty spray of arrows. This was a fatal blow to Marathas, where Mysore bowmen turned out to be lethal to handle. Sambhaji knew that most of his Maratha warriors will die if this continues, which he didn't want. So, he withdrew his army from the battlefield for the time being and camped with the army nearby. Like his father, Sambhaji was a great war strategist; seeing the challenge of dealing with the arrows of the Mysore army, he decided to take help from local cobblers. He asked cobblers to prepare leather jackets for all Maratha warriors. These jackets were not mere plain leather jackets; these jackets were customized to be laden with thick oil. On the one hand, these customized jackets were getting prepare; on the other hand, Marathas started making bows and arrows to strike Chikka Devaraja's army. Sambhaji's strategy was to bind the cloth to the arrowhead, lit it with fire, and make these arrows more deadly than Mysore's army.

Sambhaji again mobilized his army and attacked Mysore. Chikka Devaraja's army was at the top of the forts and started striking Marathas from strongholds with solid arrows. But, all their arrow attacks proved futile as oil loaded leather Jackets neutralized the arrow attacks. It was the turn of Marathas for the counter-attack, and they responded with lit arrows that were filled with gunpowder and caused blasts with every attack. These explosions caused high fatalities to the Mysore army; eventually, the forts of Mysore were captured by Marathas. This lead Chikka Devraja to sign a peace treaty to abide by the terms and conditions of Marathas.

Sambhaji had taken over the reins of the Maratha Empire. With this, he was responsible for defending the territories and defeating the enemies that his father, Shivaji, had acquired. In 1682, Sambhaji collided head-on with two powerful forces in the surrounding regions -- the Siddhis of Janjira and the Portuguese of Goa.

His first target was to capture the fort of Janjira. This was the enemy territory that had been continually fighting for power in the region. Shivaji had significantly reduced Mughal's influence in the region. Sambhaji escalated the struggle to a full-blown attack that lasted at least 30 days. However, Siddis allied with the Mughals, who attacked Raigad, and Sambhaji was forced to retreat to defend his territory. What was left behind was the loss of Maratha soldiers and an unfruitful, defeated battle.

Sambhaji prepared the counterstrategy. He marched towards the Anjadiva fort of the Portugues in verse to expand his power and territories. Although the initial siege was successful, the Marathas were later expelled from the fort by a garrison of 200 Portuguese men. Sambhaji revolted by launching an offensive campaign in Goa, which was successful to a great extent and had almost brought the Portuguese to its knees; however, Mughal intervention on both land and sea resulted in the opposing alliance to have a heavier hand. Sambhaji sought British help in 1684 to stock up his artillery and relentlessly pursued the forts along the ghats, and ultimately, Pratapgadh.

Death And Uprising Of Marathas

Mughal King Aurangzeb has ended the Adil Shahi (Shia Muslim dynasty, founded by Yusuf Adil Shah), and Qutub Shahi (dynasty ruled the Golconda Sultanate in south India). His next target was the Maratha empire. He knew to achieve the goal of finishing the Maratha empire, he should kill Sambhaji Maharaj.

Under the leadership of Hambirrao Mohite, one of Sambhaji's most celebrated counterparts in the Maratha army, the Marathas lured the Mughals into the Battle of Wai in 1687. However, the battle was considered an endpoint in Sambhaji's reign as Mohite succumbed to fatal injuries. Mohite was being hit by a cannon ball during the war. With the death of Mohite, Sambhaji's political stance was considerably weakened. Administrators cited irresponsibility and poor judgment of the second Chhatrapati as the cause.

During the 1687 post Battle of Wai, Maratha Empire was in a fragile state. They lost one of the best Commander in Chief, Hambirrao Mohite, Sambhaji's right hand. Moreover, Maratha was facing both external and internal threats.

Many Maratha Sardars started distancing themselves from the empire. Enmity was grown between Sambhaji and his brother-in-law Ganoji Shirke.

After his battalion started crumbling in the aftermath of the Battle of Wai, Sambhaji retreated towards Sangamneshwar. He was captured along with his 25 advisors by the Mughal army on the orders of Aurangzeb. Post which, he was given a brutal death in 1689. However, the accounts of how he was killed and under what circumstances vary. Mughal accounts demean Sambhaji's final days, while Maratha's accounts glorify him as the one who earned the title *Dharamveer* before being killed.

It was during February 1689 when Sambhaji Maharaj had planned for a meeting at Sangameshwar. He was always under the scanner of Ganoji Shirke, who betrayed Sambhaji by guiding Muqarrab Khan, Commander in Golconda, about the location of Sambhaji. Muqarrab Khan and his Mughal contingent of 25,000 soldiers captured Sambhaji and his men at Sangameshwar and brought him to Aurangzeb. Kavi Kalasha, the close aide of Sambhaji, was also arrested during this ambush attack by Muqarrab Khan. Pandit Kavi Kalash was the best friend and trusted advisor of Sambhaji; he was one of the close associates of Sambhaji. Chattrapati Sambhaji Maharaj has given him the post of *Chandogamatya*.

Sambhaji and Kavi Kalash were then taken to Ahmednagar, where Aurangzeb demeaned them. They were paraded in clowns cloth and were subjected to insults by Mughal soldiers. Eventually, Aurangzeb kept few conditions in front of Sambhaji to release him. He demanded to surrender all forts which Sambhaji captured from the Mughals. Aurangzeb also wanted Sambhaji to reveal conspirator's names within the Mughal army, who helped Sambhaji all this while. He also wanted Sambhaji to get converted to Islam and bow down to Aurangzeb. Sambhaji rejected all these demands and, in a fit of anger, insulted the Auragzeb.

Aurangzeb felt insulted, and he ordered to kill Sambhaji. In the process, he was tortured for over a fortnight. Sambhaji's eyes and tongue were plucked out, nails were pulled out, and skin was removed. Finally, on 11th March 1689, he was killed. His body was thrown at Tulapur on the Banks of Bhima River, which is near Pune. The Maratha king was tortured inhumanly and was finally executed. Sambhaji Maharaj became a Dharmaveer.

Sambhaji's cruel death by Aurangzeb was the turning point of the Maratha empire as many Sardars who moved out of the Maratha empire returned. This incident ignited anger and self-respect in Marathas. The Marathas gave a tough fight to the Mughals. They fought to their last breath to keep Maratha's honor intact. The killing of Chhatrapati Sambhaji had infuriated the Marathas. However, the war would endure with transformed energy.

Meanwhile, Sambhaji's son Shahu was held captive until the early 1700s, when he was finally released with the ulterior motive of sowing seeds of internal conflicts.

Chapter 25

Santaji Ghorpade

"Attack Which Could Have Changed The History"

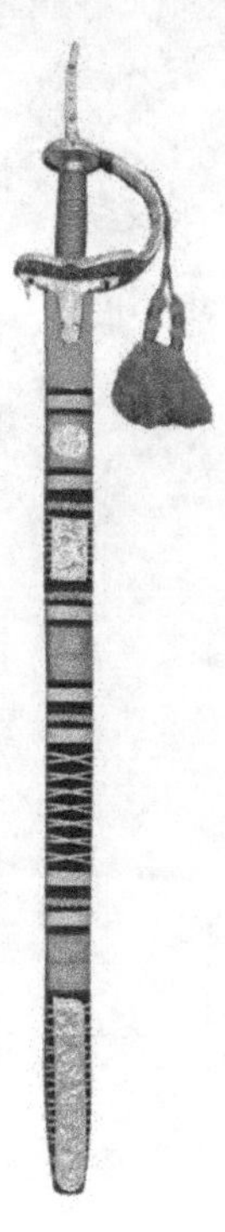

Santaji was one of the greatest Commander in Chief in the Maratha army under Rajaram. He had bettered his father Maloji Ghorpade, commander in chief during Sambhaji Maharaj rule. Santaji is considered one of the notable experts of Guerilla warfare.

Sambhaji's cruel killing by Aurangzeb has made every Maratha angry. They wanted to take revenge from the Mughals. Santaji wished to take revenge and decided to attack Aurangzeb. For Marathas, it wasn't just a clash for provincial sovereignty anymore. For them, it was a war for the victory of *Dharma* over *Adharma*. This was a war for the triumph of honor. So, Marathas under Santaji Ghorpade, decided to attack the Mughals to hit Mughal forces very hard, physically and emotionally.

During that time, Aurangzeb had camped between Tulapur and Koregaon. He was planning to travel to Chakan. Santaji Ghorpade decided to attack Aurangzeb's camp. Santaji had his trusted spies all around, and he ensured that he gets every minute detail of Aurangzeb's camp promptly. This helped him to make his attack effective. Spies provided all the camp details, including total guards and their timings of keeping watch of the base, actual number, size of tents, total assets held in the camp, etc. Aurangzeb's quarters in the tent were known as *"Daulat Khana,"* and he resided in this tent during Camping.

Many Maratha soldiers were too in Aurangzeb's army, and Santaji decided to use this as a source to enter Aurangzeb's camp. Santaji reached the base and convinced Mughal guards that they were part of Aurangzeb's army. Santaji and his army entered the camp, started slaughtering Mughal troops, and made their way to the Royal tent.When Santaji entered *"Daulat Khana,"* to his disappointment, he could not find Aurangzeb there. Luck was on the Mughal emperor's side that he escaped the deadly attack from Maratha warriors. Many of Aurangzeb's private forces and bodyguards were slaughtered that night. Even though Aurangzeb had survived, the message from this attack was clear: Sambhaji may have been killed, but Marathas will continue to fight for honor till they succeed.

Maratha warriors lead by Santaji ensured all tent ropes are cut. The entire camp of the Mughal army was crashed down within no time. Marathas destroyed the whole camp of Mughals. However, they could not get hold of Aurangzeb, but this deadly attack ensured many causalities in Mughal's army. Santaji then flew away from the camp and reached Sinhagad. He was not happy with the result of the Koregaon attack as he could not kill Aurangzeb.

The attack on Aurangzeb camp was successful. However, this attack could have changed history had it reached the desired result planned by Santaji, which was the killing of Aurangzeb.

Post this attack, he reached Panhala and appraised Rajaram about his campaign of attacking Aurangzeb's tent. This was one of the bravest attacks by Marathas, and Santaji was honored with the title *"Mamlakat Madar."*

Chapter 26
Chhatrapati Rajaram Maharaj
"Asylum By Keladi Chennamma"

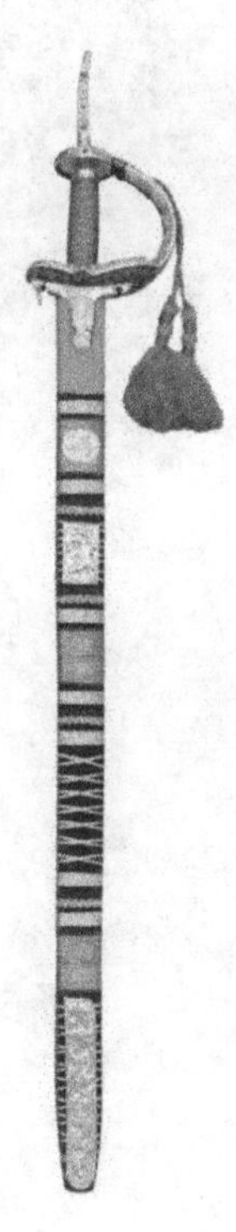

Anticipating Mughal attacks on the Maratha territory with the ruler being killed by the Mughal Emperor, Rajaram quickly assumed his position as the third Chhatrapati on 12th March 1689. Thus began his reign. However, within a couple of weeks, the Mughals attacked Raigad to capture Rajaram and end the Maratha empire.

This led to the battle of Raigad in 1689, led by the Mughal general Zulfikar Khan against the young Maratha ruler. With the support of his loyal ministers and relatives, Rajaram commanded the Maratha army to put up a brave fight. At the same time, he made his escape to the fort of Gingee through the forts of Pratapgadh and Vishalgadh. In this event, a figure of special significance was Keladi Chennamma, the ferocious queen from Karnataka who fought the battle against the Mughals being at the forefront and helped Rajaram safe escape. The struggle stretched far too long for the Mughals to preserve their pride and created history as they signed a peace accord for the first time with an Indian ruler, Chennamma. Another attempt was made to capture Rajaram with an attack on Gingee that failed as the Maratha ruler successfully escaped to Vellore.

After Sambhaji Maharaj's death, Rajaram was crowned as Chhatrapati; he was the younger son of Shivaji Maharaj and half-brother of Sambhaji Maharaj. The Mughals humiliated and killed Sambhaji; they thought that the Maratha empire is now finished. However, that was not the case. Rajaram was made the next Chhatrapati of the Maratha empire. Marathas sent a loud and clear message to Mughals that Maratha Empire still existed and will give a good fight to their enemies. Post coronation, it was decided that Rajaram will fight the Mughals his way out to different strongholds. Rajaram Maharaj chose to move to Gingee. This was the start of an escape that would finally see him travel to Gingee fort in faraway Tamil Nadu. Aurangzeb, who knew that Rajaram will go to Gingee hence was determined to capture Rajaram. This would have ensured that the Maratha empire is finished from the roots. By now, Aurangzeb had captured Raigad, Panhala, and other vital forts of Marathas. He wanted to swallow the entire Maharashtra by capturing/killing Rajaram. He ordered a strict vigil on all the routes to Gingee to ensure Rajaram is captured by Mughals.

During his journey of survival, Rajaram approached many Kingdoms for shelter. Still, most of them refused as they didn't want to take enmity with Aurangzeb. Finally, one day Rajaram reached a place in the Keladi Kingdom, which is in Karnataka. Queen Keladi Chennamma was ruling the Keladi Kingdom then.

Every afternoon Queen Keladi Chennamma gave alms to the needy; she saw few Sadhus standing in a queue who looked very radiant. Queen knew that they are not ordinary Sadhus. Group of Sadhus waited till all the others had received their alms, and once their turn came, their leader saluted Queen.

Seeing this, Queen said in a polite voice, "Sadhu Maharaj, you should bless me and not salute me. Let me know how I can serve you?"

The leader of Sadhus came forward and said, "Great Queen Keladi Chennamma, we are not the Sadhus. I am Maharaj Rajaram of the Maratha Kingdom and Son of Chhatrapati Shivaji Maharaj"

After hearing this, Queen was astonished; she respected Shivaji Maharaj a lot. But, she was surprised to see Shivaji's son in this condition. Rajaram then explained all incidents, including Sambhaji Maharaj's killing and; how he escaped the Mughals and planning to capture Gingee. Finally, he requested shelter in Keladi.

Queen Keladi Chennamma was known for her bravery and taking bold decisions to protect her people and belief. She knew that all other kings have denied shelter to Rajaram, and it can be lethal to take enmity with Mughals. But Queen decided to extend her support to Rajaram.

She discussed this request of Rajaram with her ministers.

Most of the ministers were in the opinion of not providing shelter to Rajaram as Mughals have taken down the Maratha Kingdom post-Sambhaji's death. However, overruling the majority's view, Queen Chennamma decided to give shelter to Rajaram. The message reached loud and clear to Aurangzeb that Keladi will draw a war with the Mughals. Aurungzeb sent his army to Keladi for a battle. However, under Queen Keladi Chennamma's headship, the attacks were effectively resisted. Keladi's army also captured many Mugal officers during this war. This was a commendable achievement at a time when the Mughals were very dominant.

Once Rajaram escaped out of Keladi, he moved towards Gingee, which is now in Tamil Nadu. This was the center of the Maratha Kingdom in the Deccan. Finally, in 1689 Rajaram reached Gingee fort with his entourage and ended the epic of his voyages. Rajaram received the grand welcome in Gingee by Marathas, and it was the new beginning of the Maratha empire. It puffed new life into a struggle that seemed all but lost for the Marathas.

Queen Keladi Chennamma played a crucial role in the Maratha empire. She went ahead for war with the Mughals and helped escape Rajaram, who eventually revitalized the Maratha empire. Queen Keladi Chennamma's courageous choice was to give asylum for Rajaram, which paved the way for the Maratha Kingdom to gain their freedom from the Mughals.

Rajaram's reign was a dubious one with resilient uncertainty over the power struggles for the control of Deccan between the Mughals and the Marathas. Back-to-back blows with the death of some of the fiercest soldiers were breaking the back of this empire. In yet another battering blow, Rajaram, Shivaji's younger son, succumbed to lung disease and died in 1700.

The news of weakening Maratha's power and the absence of a contemptible successor to continue the legacy spread like wildfire. It was an enormous relief to Aurangzeb. They believed it was finally time to throttle the Maratha menace and take over control of the Deccan; however, the unexpected happened. Rajaram's widow, queen Tarabai assessed the crumbling situation and took over incumbency to stand firm against the Mughal forces.

Chapter 27

Queen Tarabai

“The Unflagging Warrior Queen”

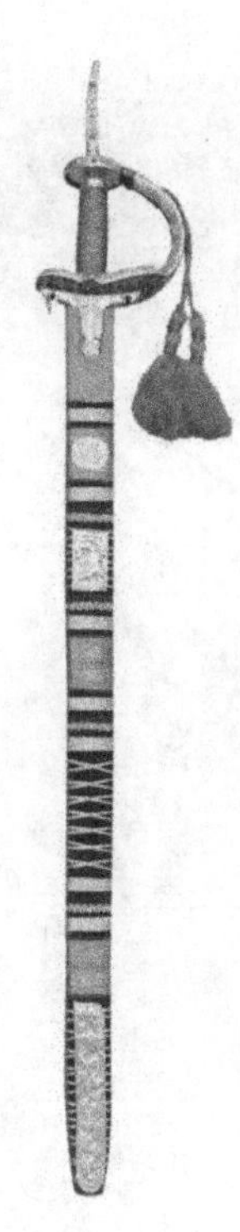

Rajaram and Tarabai's son Shivaji II was only four years old when Queen Tarabai took control as a regent. Shivaji II was throned as the fourth Chhatrapati. Tarabai was a highly influential advisor in civil, diplomatic, and even military matters during Rajaram's rule. Tarabai was influential in saving the Maratha empire from collapse.

Her husband became the Chhatrapati once Shambhaji was killed by Aurangzeb. Rajaram and Tarabai were forced to move out of Rajgad by Mughals. They reached Gingee fort in Tamil Nadu; it was the southernmost part of the Maratha empire. This was the safest choice for Rajaram. However, the Mughals kept following Rajaram, and Zulfiqar Ali Khan was leading this mission. Zulfiqar sieged the Gingee fort, but little he knew that this siege will be one of the longest sieges in Mughal history. The blockade went for almost 8 years, from 1690 to 1698. These 8 years were difficult for Marathas, and any wrong decision would mean the end of the Maratha empire. During this time, Rajaram's health started deteriorating. It was Tarabai who showed her leadership quality and pioneer to take the Maratha legacy ahead. She controlled the Gingee fort, but she also commanded and executed the fight against Mughals outside Tamil Nadu and Maharashtra.

Eventually, in 1698 Rajaram and Tarabai managed to escape out of the fort and returned to Maharashtra. In 1700 Rajaram passed away. Tarabai was only 25-year-old that time. The crisis was on, and if not appropriately managed, the Maratha Empire would have collapsed. During this catastrophe, Tarabai became the supreme guiding force for Maratha. Her administrative skills and strong character saved the *Swarajya*. Her strategy was to precalculate Aurangzeb's strategy. She predicted his moves before he had the time to elaborately plan them and made aggressive counter-strategies. She rebuilt the Maratha's power towards the offensive and began reconsolidating territories towards the north. It was under her leadership that the Marathas successfully raided Malwa and Gujarat to strengthen their economy. Her formidable strength and ingenious cavalry and administrative skills saved the Maratha empire from disintegrating.

Tarabai's grit and power had started threatening Mughal pride. She aggressively expanded territory and fiercely defended her forts. At the same time, Shivaji II grew up to become a brave warrior, just like his mother. The Mughals staged another attack on the stronghold of Raigad. This led to the battle of Raigad in 1704. This battle saw complete vandalization of the fortress and a painful loss of power for the Marathas.

Tarabai endured firmly at the control from 1700-07. Even her enemies praised her courage and brave tactics; as per her enemies' words, "Tarabai showed great supremacies of expertise and governance. Each day, the war spread and the control of the Marathas augmented."

Tarabai had her eyes set on the goal of overthrowing Mughals from the Deccan and capturing absolute power in the north. Although she was not successful in killing her Mughal rival. The Marathas were jubilant with the death of Aurangzeb due to mortal illness in 1707 in Aurangabad, a city in present-day Maharashtra.

Beneath Tarabai's rule, the Maratha army established their rule over Southern Karnataka and raided several affluent towns of the state's western coast, such as Surat, Burhanpur, Broach, etc.

This decade marked another internal conflict and power struggle for the throne of the Chhatrapati between two step-brothers; Shahu, the son of Sambhaji, and Shivaji II, the son of Rajaram. The Mughals were aware of the insatiable power hunger and easy rivalries between stepbrothers inside the Maratha royal family. Taking advantage of which they decided to set Sambhaji's son Shahu free as another decisive blow.

The Marathas had little time to celebrate. Mughals had

already played their card by sending back Shahu to the Empire, which would have otherwise been another news of joy, had he not gone on to declare war on the then Chhatrapati and his stepbrother, Shivaji II.

Tarabai died in 1761 when she was 86, few months after the third Battle of Panipat where Ahmad Shah Abdali overwhelmed the Maratha Army. Had the unconquerable queen Tarabai not taken control of the Maratha empire in 1700, then probably Marathas would have faced downfall much earlier, and the history of India would have been different.

Chapter 28
Chhatrapati Shahu Maharaj
"Raja Of Satara"

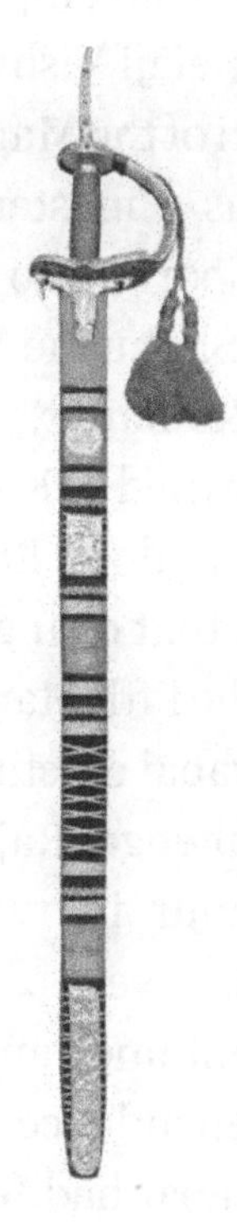

In 1707 when Aurangzeb died, his son, Azam released Shahu, Shivaji Maharaj's son. The idea was to create a succession war within Marathas. However, Shahu's mother, Yesubai, wife Savitribai, and half-brother Madan Singh remained imprisoned with Mughals as insurance against Shahu's good act against Mughals. Indeed, queen Tarabai rejected Shahu's claim to the throne of the Maratha empire. However, few Marathas joined Shahu. Among them, Balaji Vishwanath played a crucial role in making Shahu a Chattrapati of the Maratha kingdom.

Balaji Vishwanath was a master strategist; he was able to bring many of Tarabai's supporters to Shahu's camp. Eventually, Tarabai had to agree to make Shahu the Maratha King. In return, she got an individual kingdom of Kolhapur.

In 1708 Shahu was crowned as King of Maratha kingdom with Satara as the Capital of the kingdom. Shahu's successful revolt was followed by a series of events that changed the demographics of the royal reign. The crowning of the fifth Maratha Chhatrapati as Shahu I in 1708 resulted in Queen Tarabai erecting her kingdom in Kolhapur as a sign of rebellion and challenge. Rajaram II, Tarabai's son, was declared the Raja of Kolhapur in 1710, where he reigned and succumbed to smallpox within 4 years. Being the direct successor of Shivaji Maharaj, Shahu was untamed and menacing when it came to territorial conflicts and independence. He fiercely fought for the Marathas. Unlike Queen Tarabai had feared, his time spent under the Mughal supervision and captivity only helped him customize his battle tactics with insider information. This drastically helped him expand Maratha's power far and wide.

In the years following Shivaji's death and killing of Sambhaji, Shahu Maharaj had started to restructure itself after Aurangzeb's death in 1707.

Shahu Maharaj was the first Chhatrapati with a reign of over 15 years and a renowned one at that. During his time, one power shift that Shahu instrumentalized changed Maratha's history in terms of rulers and ruling powers; Balaji Vishwanath was appointed as his Peshwa by Shahu Maharaj. He bestowed significant influences in his hands, thus starting a fire to the legacy of the Peshwas. They indelibly escalated the integrity and sovereignty of the Maratha empire for decades to come.

Expansion And Distribution Of Maratha Power Under Chhatrapati Shahu Maharaj

The decade saw the continued rule and consolidation of power under the leadership of Chhatrapati Shahu Maharaj and his chief minister, one of his most trusted, Peshwa Balaji Vishwanath. During this time, the powers of Peshwas increased, and they went on to assume the highest positions in administrative rankings and defenders of the Maratha confederacy. Thus, it was the foundation of new Maratha power. Maratha empire was set to see its rule and acquisition peak. This happened with formidable leaders forming the pillars on all sides of the subcontinent.

In 1719 Mughal emperor Rafi-ud-Darajat gave rights of *Chauth* and *Sardeshmukhi* of six Mughal subas to Chhatrapati Shahu Maharaj. In return, Marathas would maintain an army of 15000 Maratha soldiers to protect the Mughal emperor.

This decade also gave power to the Greatest known ruler that the Marathas and India had ever seen, Baji Rao.

Maratha Empire Capital

When Shivaji Maharaj was formally crowned as Chhatrapati in 1674, he made Raigad a capital of the Maratha Empire. When Shambaji Maharaj became Chhatrapati, he continued Raigad as the capital of the empire.

Things started changing when Rajaram became Chhatrapati. There were regular threats from Mughals of capturing Raigad; hence capital has shifted Sinhgad Fort for a while. As Rajaram was at Gingee fort, Gingee became a temporary capital for the empire.

After the death of Rajaram Maharaj, there were power conflicts between Shahu Maharaj (son of Sambhaji) and Tarabai (wife of Rajaram). By then, Raigad lost its importance as the Maratha Empire's capital. The dispute between Shahu Maharaj and Tarabai was settled in 1731 as part of the Treaty of Warna. The Maratha empire was divided into two kingdoms, Satara and Kolhapur.

Later, when Shahu Maharaj gave the military power to Peshwas, the Pune got importance as the capital of the Maratha empire relatively than Satara.

Chapter 29
Kanhoji Angre
"Samundra Datta Shivaji"

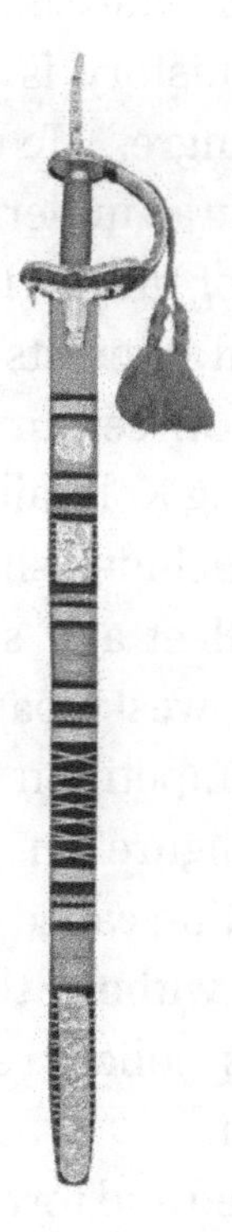

If we go through the great empires of *Bharat*, most of them used the sea primarily for trade and richness. Most of them didn't realize the potential sea holds for a military base and commercial activity. However, during the late 17th and 18th centuries, when European colonialism emerged, one Maratha warrior arose along the Konkan coast as the native sovereignty defender over coastal seawater, and he was Kanhoji Angre. Whenever Maratha history is referred to, one name will always be evoked "Kanhoji Angre." He was appointed as *Sarkhel* or admiral by the chief of Satara; under that authority, he was the master of the western coast of India. He fought against the British, Dutch, and Portuguese naval interests on the Indian coast during more significant parts of the 18th century.

Kanhoji grew up among Koli sailors and learned seamanship from them; his fleet mainly included ships engineered by Kolis. The combination of his unique fleet and strategic mind established a fearsome authority on the west coast. Through his admirable techniques, he gave tough competition to the British. As a result, he became the most dreaded figure on the Konkan coast. He also imposed a system of registration called *Dastaks* and seized any ship traveling in Konkan waters without them. The European powers refused to comply with this policy, resulting in conflict between Khahoji Angre and the British.

In 1710, Angre captured and fortified the Kandhir islands and fiercely fought the British vessel Godolphin. In 1713, 10 forts were ceded by the British to Angre owing to his resilience and fervor. To ensure smooth trade, the East India Company decided to sign a peace treaty with Kanhoji. He agreed, thereby granting them permission to access and enter Konkan waters. However, the peace hardly lasted two years before Charles Boone, the new Governor-General of Bombay, arrived. He made several failed attempts to capture Kanhoji Angre and instead ended up losing his ships to Kanhoji. This vehemently angered the British, which led to the attack on Vijaydurg in 1720, Kanhoji's first base. Still, they couldn't stand long against the great warrior that Kanhoji was. Despite their battered pride and naval defense conditions, in another attempt, the British and Portuguese joined forces attacked Alibagh in 1721. Only to be vanquished and being unsuccessful in causing any damage to the exploding Maratha power.

Kanhoji's undefeatable valor and grit came to be renowned far and wide, earning him the prestigious title of *Samundra Datta Shivaji.*

Peshwa Tree (Post Balaji Vishwanath)

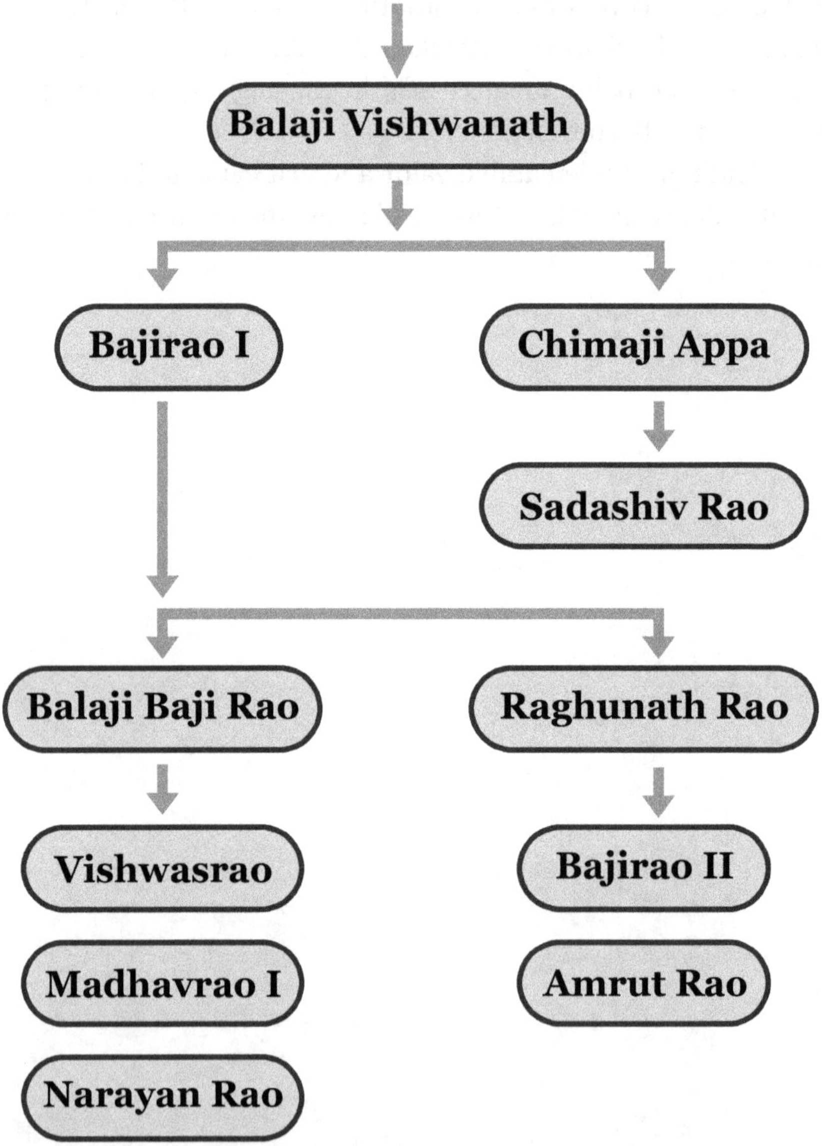

- Balaji Vishwanath
  - Bajirao I
    - Balaji Baji Rao
      - Vishwasrao
      - Madhavrao I
      - Narayan Rao
    - Raghunath Rao
      - Bajirao II
      - Amrut Rao
  - Chimaji Appa
    - Sadashiv Rao

Chapter 30
Balaji Vishwanath
"Second Founder Of The Maratha Empire"

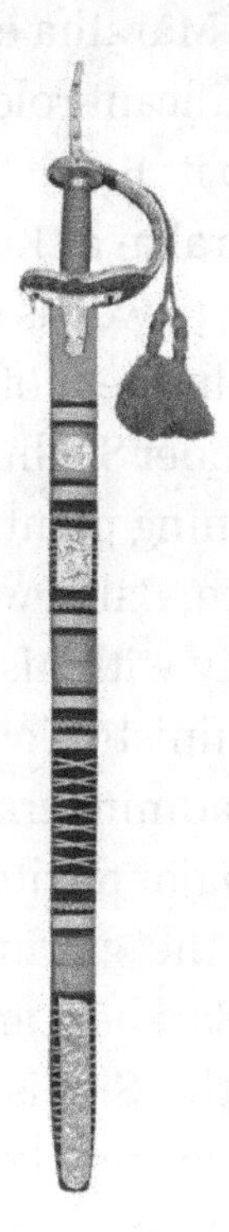

Balaji Vishwanath was born on January 1st, 1662, in Shrivardhan, Maharashtra. He was the sixth Peshwa and the first in a series of inherited Peshwas of the Maratha empire. Balaji started his journey in the Maratha empire as an accountant. He worked as Maratha administration for Maratha General Dhanaji Jadhav. Balaji Vishwanath was the key person who influenced Dhanaji Jadhav to support Shahu (son of Sambhaji Maharaj) when he was released by the Mughals from their captivity.

The civil war that erupted between Tarabai and Shahu Maharaj at the throne of the Maratha empire was gaining impetus. Balaji Vishwanath had a significant role in fueling the war and then ultimately bringing an end to it. Balaji Vishwanath helped Shahu to raise the army and defeat Tarabai at Kolhapur. 1712 resulted in the fall of Tarabai as an opposing power as she fell prey to Balaji's coup, which further led to the appointment of Sambhaji II at the throne of Kolhapur as a dummy ruler under Shahu.

This was a crucial turning point in how the Maratha empire would take shape in the future. Balaji was a great strategist and had many victories under his kitty with his negotiation tactics. He was best in court politics and administration. Balaji Vishwanath utilized his increased military and administrative powers to brave away external forces and capture major territories in the external aspect of things. Joining hands with the glorious name of Maratha navy, Kanhoji Angre, the newly Sarkhel, and Balaji became a unique combination that defeated the Siddis of Janjira. These qualities helped him to the position as the first Peshwa of the Maratha empire in November 1713. With the responsibility of Peshwa came certain powers, and Balaji Vishwanath utilized his skills to consolidate the Maratha empire and brought many disputing factions under one empire. This is one of the reasons he is called the second founder of the Maratha state. To appease the Maratha Sardars, Balaji introduced the *Jagirdari* system. He created a co-operative commission for all Maratha Sardars and appointed Chhatrapati Shahu, the commission's head. This is how Peshwa assumed utmost importance, with Chhatrapati turning to be a nominal ruler only.

Peshwa Balaji braced the then Emperor Farrukhsiyar's attacks and progressed towards their ultimate goal of disposing of the Mughals from Delhi. He defended and overturned several attacks made by Mughal Viceroys which led to them signing a peace treaty with Balaji. In 1718, this treaty negotiated Mughals agreeing to give one-fourth of their revenues of the ancient Mughal provinces in the Deccan region under Maratha control to the Marathas. This revenue came to be known as *Chauth*--a notable diplomatic victory for the Shivaji legacy. However, associating with the same Viceroy sent to reclaim the Deccan, due to Farrykhsiyar's resistance to the treaty, Balaji and Syed Hussain Ali Khan colluded to overthrow the Emperor. With massive military support from the Marathas, Hussain Ali Khan managed to snatch away the throne. Thereby marking Maratha's hegemony and supreme influence over the throne of Delhi by 1719.

In 1720, after the death of the valiant warrior Balaji Vishwanath, the Peshwa legacy was succeeded by his son, Baji Rao. In the next 20 years, along with the then Chhatrapati Shahu Maharaj, Baji Rao became the supreme Indian warrior of all time.

Chapter 31

Baji Rao Peshwa

"The Zenith Of The Maratha Empire"

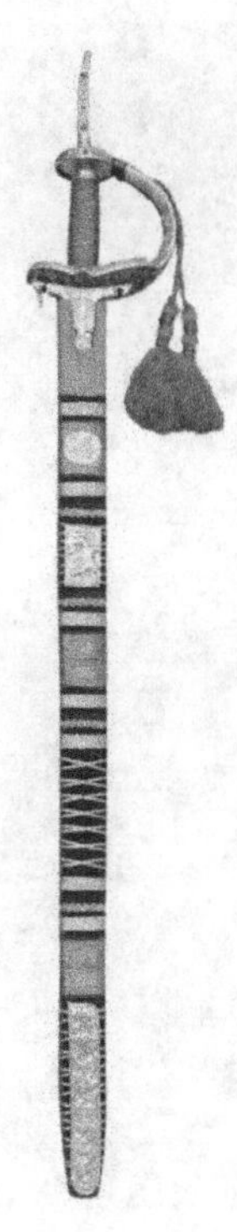

Baji Rao was born on 18th August 1700; he was the eldest son of Peshwa Balaji Vishwanath Rao. Baji Rao, like his father, was the critical warrior who took "Peshwaship" to the next level. Since childhood, Baji Rao has had a very close association with his father. He always accompanied his father during military campaigns. This was hands-on training for Baji Rao in military tactics. Peshwa Balaji Vishwanath, the father of Baji Rao, played a similar role to him played by Jijaji (mother of Shivaji Maharaj) in Chhatrapati Shivaji Maharaj's life.

In April 1720, When Peshwa Balaji Vishwanath passed away, Maharaja Shahu appointed Baji Rao as the next Peshwa.

The battle with the Nizams became a frontline focus in 1721, right after Baji Rao assumed the position as Peshwa. The Nizam-el-Mulk, Asaf Jah I, viewed the Marathas as hurdles in his conquest to instate his reign over the whole of Deccan regions. He had launched his operations two times in a short period to win over the Maratha regions. Still, he and his army had to retreat on both occasions. Finally, in 1727, with the help of Sambhaji II, he invaded Pune and, in return, made him the Chhatrapati and left the province.

Meanwhile, Baji Rao, who was cognizant of Nizam's intentions, took advantage of his absence. Using the battalion of Pindaris, he employed the technique of guerrilla warfare. Baji Rao started plotting fierce and rampant attacks on the cities ruled by the Nizam. He began from Jalna and Sindkhed, annihilated as many areas as possible, and then marched forward to Chhota Udaipur in Gujarat. There, he strategically, with the intent to deceive Asaf, bluffed about moving towards Burhanpur, which, he knew, was of utmost strategic importance to the Nizam. The Nizam, with the counter-intent to meet Baji Rao, set off towards Burhanpur. He and Baji Rao came face to face at Palkhed and was quickly outwitted by the Maratha army. Ultimately Nizam was left with no plausible alternative but to sign a treaty to maintain accord.

The battle of Palkhed was fought in 1728 between Baji Rao Peshwa and Nizam.

This Battle of Palkhed, which several historians and scholars described as a brilliant combination of military science and battle tactics, was a classic strategic brainchild of Baji Rao, the Peshwa, and concluded during the early months of 1728.

The early 1730s marked the fresh struggles of the Marathas with the Siddis of Janjira and Gujarat forces.

Baji Rao wanted to expand Maratha territory to collect tax from the province of Gujarat. However, he faced a revolt from Trimbak Rao Dabhade. Baji Rao had to battle against the alliance, which consisted of Muhammad Khan Bangash, Nizam, and Sambhaji II. In the battle of Dabhol, Baji Rao defeated and killed Trimbak Rao Dabhade. The Marathas emerged victoriously and concorded with the Dabhade clan to share half of the revenue. The Siddis, on the other hand, were too obstinate to refrain from launching an attack to consolidate their powers in the Raigad, Rewas, Thal, and Chaul territories of the Marathas. Chimaji, the younger brother of Baji Rao, retorted by instilling an attack on their base camp and forcing them to sign a treaty to set clear boundaries for them.

The Chhtrassals from Bundelkhand had formed an independent rule by deposing the Mughals from that region. However, incessant attacks led to them seeking assistance from Baji Rao. As soon as Baji Rao was successful with his Malwa campaign, in 1729, he joined hands with Chhatrassals during their captivity under Khan Bangash. Pilaji Jadhav, Dawalji Somwanshi, and Tukoji Pawar are some of the most revered warriors who fought with the Mughals in this region. Their massive army attacked Bangash in Jaitpur. Although they couldn't throttle Bangash's forces, his son Qaim Khan was defeated. Bangash was coerced out with an agreement of never returning to Bundelkhand.

With the splurge of unprecedented victory, Baji Rao had earned the name of the 'warrior who never lost a single battle.' The entire subcontinent was hoisted with saffron flags. Signifying the magnanimous rise of the Maratha Empire and its glorious expansion to the north and south. This decade marked the final phase of capturing Delhi and other vital territories to claim Maratha power as the sole supreme power in Hindustan.

Baji Rao Proceeds To Acquire Delhi

In an unpredicted series of events in November 1736, Baji Rao marched to Delhi with ferocious audacity and initial intentions of atrocity in mind. He wanted to prove a point to the Mughals and instill fear in the minds of an already disintegrating empire. To check the Maratha movement before reaching Delhi, Saadat Khan was appointed to restrict the crusade of the Maratha cavalry of 50,000 beyond the Yamuna river. The battle was baffling despite the clear outnumbered soldiers with Malhar Rao Holkar and Pilaji Jadhav at the forefront. However, Holkar managed to join Baji Rao to fight the primary cause. The Mughals, who were overjoyed on having trampled a Maratha plan, were baffled on learning that this was a mere strategy to distract them. The entire Maratha army had taken the jungle root through Jats and Mewatis to reach Delhi.

The Battle of Delhi in 1737 that ensued was an open challenge of Maratha's expansion towards the north. Although Baji Rao retreated to Pune, his purpose was fulfilled with the Mughal Emperor Muhammad Shah feeling terrified of the Maratha threat. Therefore, Shah conspired with Nizams and the Nawabs to take over the Deccan-based rulers. This alliance resulted in the Battle of Bhopal in 1737; Baji Rao strategized this war similar to the tactics of Palkhed. It led to the pivotal victory of the Marathas over the triple allied forces. This resulted in the Nizams ceding over the entire Malwa and the territories between Narbada and Chambal and millions of rupees worth war fine.

Combat With The Portugues

Towards the end of the decade, Baji Rao also undertook missions of defending the Portugues further beyond Indian territories by taking over the fort of Ghodbunder. With the support of Manaji Angre, he managed to capture regions of Bandra, Dharavi, Versova while Chimaji Appa, his brother, held tight near Vasai. With most areas around Vasai under Maratha's control, they besieged the Vasai Fort in May 1739.

Baji Rao, Chimaji Appa, Holkar, and Scindia fought a pitched battle against the Portuguese with a scavenging spirit of destruction until the fort hoisted the Maratha flag. The battle of Vasai lasted 13 days since the breach of the Sao Sebastiao towers. It ended on 16th May with the Portuguese governor's surrender, marking a triumphant victory for Baji Rao, unfortunately, one of his last.

Peshwa Bajirao died on 28th April 1740. It is said that he died of a rapid fever. During that time, he was traveling towards Delhi along with Maratha troops and camping in the district of Khargon, at present near Indore city. He was incinerated at Raverkhedi on the river Narmada. The Scindias built a *chhatri* as a commemorative at this place. The untimely death of Peshwa Baji Rao I in 1740 proved to be the most tremendous loss of the Maratha empire.

Constant historic victories of Baji Rao made him the great warrior in Indian history. Every success reflected his clever battle tactics, massive territorial expansions, and wisdom in diplomatic resolutions. This accelerated the rise of the Marathas up to its hilt. Finally, the dream of *Hindavi Swarajya* was close to becoming a reality.

Chapter 32
Chimaji Appa
"Capture Of Vasai Fort"

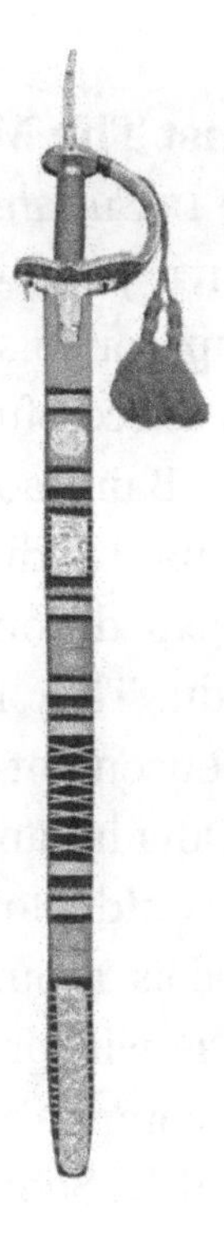

Chimaji Appa, born in 1706, was the younger brother of Great Baji Rao Peshwa. He barely lived for 34 years. However, in the short span of life, he achieved so much for the Maratha kingdom that his contribution, when compared, can equalize the contribution of Great Baji Rao Peshwa. Chimaji Appa played a crucial role in defeating the Portuguese by capturing the Vasai fort.

The Campaign Against The Malwa Began In 1723

Malwa was one of the 12 *Subahs* designated by the Mughals specifically for administrative purposes. Girdhar Bahadur was employed by the Mughal emperor to shield the *Subah* against the Marathas. They were already successful in collecting tax or *Chauth* from the south Malwa region. Baji Rao delegated a battalion to his younger brother, Chimaji Appa. Leading a massive army, Chimaji marked the beginning of the expedition in October. Maratha troops crossed the gates near Mandu. They halted near Nalchha after a month and a half of the commencement of the mission.

Meanwhile, Girdhar Bahadur and Daya Bahadur (his cousin) realized that the Marathas could plot an attack. So they began initiating the military protocols around the ghat near Amjhera, speculating that the Marathas will probably descend from there. However, the Marathas had a competitive advantage due to the light horsemen's ability to move swiftly. Soon Girdhar Bahadur was taken aback that the army of Marathas riding horses was coming straight towards them.

The 1728 face-off between both the forces in the battle of Amjhera was formidable. But, soon, the army led by Chimaji had outweighed the Mughal army, assassinated both the brothers, captured their artillery, and rampaged their base camp. The news of the triumph had proliferated like wildfire. Chimaji received applause for his meritorious accomplishment.

Portuguese, who came to India around the 16th century, was a well-known power holder in the Kokan area; they built many forts to defend their territory. All their forts were occupied with modern artillery and guns to protect the forts from enemies. Portuguese always had an expansion plan in their mind. As part of this strategy, they started building a massive fortress at Thane across the slimmest part of a stream that detached the mainland from the island of Sashti north of Bombay. This fort was the last entry point into Sashti. When Marathas came to know about this move of the Portuguese, they decided to act immediately before the fort is built and ruled by the Portuguese. In March 1737, Chimaji Appa reached Konkan and captured the incomplete fort and island of Sashti. This was a significant blow to the Portuguese by Maratha.

Chimaji continued his attack on the Portuguese. This time, Maratha attacked the fort of Vasai, which was located near Ulhas river bay. This was uniquely surrounded by the rivers from three sides and had immense walls and towers to protect it from invaders. The first attempt of Marathas to capture Vasai fort failed. As a result of this, they had several casualties and had to abandon the mission. During this time, Chimaji Appa had to leave the Vasai campaign and head north to the Tapi river to help Baji Rao Peshwa campaign against the Nizam. This campaign was won by Baji Rao.

Chimaji was a fighter and never gave up quickly on anything. His mind was clear; he wanted to capture Vasai fort. In 1739 he attacked the fortress of Vasai with his army. Chimaji Appa, along with many Maratha chiefs, gathered in the Konkan. They all were determined to eradicate oppressive Portuguese power in the area. Strategically one army unit was sent towards Goa to block any rescue support by the Viceroy to Vasai fort for the Portuguese army. Thus, the campaign to conquer Vasai began. The forts at Bandra, Versova, Thane, and Tarapur were captured by Marathas. Now, the battle of Vasai began between Marathas and the Portuguese.

The fight between two armies went on till 4 days, all these days air was filled with sounds of swords and boom of mines and; cannons. Non-stop firing from the fort caused heavy casualties to Marathas. However, Chimaji Appa and the Maratha army refused to withdraw. Finally, the Portuguese surrendered, and the Vasai fort was captured by Chimaji Appa. He was principled in victory; thus, the Portuguese were given a safe passage to evacuate the fort.

The battle of Vasai is a crucial phase of the Maratha empire. Post this victory, a peace of agreement was signed between Marathas and the Portuguese Viceroy at Goa. This was a moral victory for Marathas and a significant blow to the Portuguese's reputation. The only control left with the Portuguese was the province of Goa.

Chimaji Appa died in 1740. It was due to health issues. His legacy was taken ahead by his son Sadashivrao Bhau who fought the war of Panipat against Ahmad Shah Abdali.

Chapter 33
Peshwa Balaji Baji Rao
"Nana Saheb"

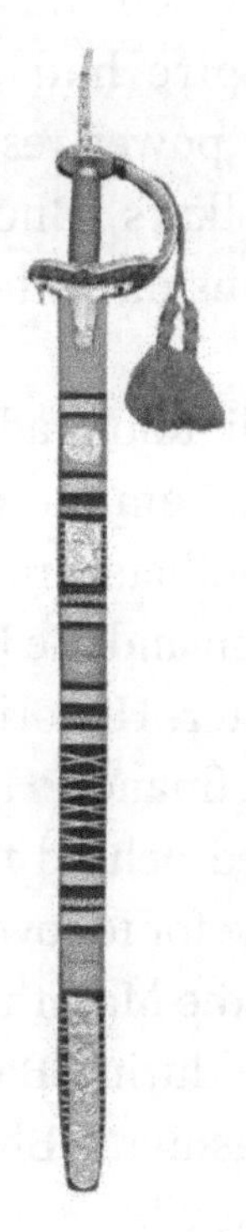

With Baji Rao leaving a seemingly indestructible legacy behind, his son Balaji Baji Rao was bestowed with the prodigious responsibility of taking it forward. During this time, the power with major influence among Marathas was with the Peshwas, while Chhatrapati Shahu Maharaj was merely an emperor on the throne. Peshwa Balaji Baji Rao, also known as Nana Saheb, was the eighth Peshwa of the Maratha empire. The empire had transformed into a tight confederacy with maximum power residing in the hands of chief executive generals like Holkars, Bhonsles, and Scindias. This resulted in a mammoth expansion of the Maratha territories due to their efforts.

Under Peshwa Balaji Rao's administration, the Maratha empire struggled with the emancipated kingdom they had established. As a result, conflicts arose internally, with Tarabai building an opposing rebellion and the Rajput's withdrawal, leaving several eminent warriors bitter. Historical records state that Balaji Baji Rao had great finesse in finance. However, his battle skills and strategic war planning lacked behind the mighty footsteps of Baji Rao I, that he was responsible for following. All these resulted in the beginning of the downfall of the Maratha empire. Many judicial and revenue reforms were made during Balaji Rao's tenure; however, credit goes to his cousin Sadashivrao Bhau(Chimaji Appa's son) and his subordinate Balshastri Gadgil.

In 1751, Balaji Baji Rao launched an offensive attack on the territories of the Nizams, and despite having to retreat due to fierce allied opposition, he persisted in 1752. The entire scuffle was to replace the current Nizam Salabat Jung with Ghazi ud-Din Khan, who had bribed the Marathas of a hefty sum, among other favors. However, since Khan soon succumbed to poisoning, a peace treaty was formed between the Nizams and the Marathas. This was a paradigm shift after the several battles that Balaji's father had fought and won against them.

The Jatts and Marathas had peaceful relations in the North. However, Suraj Mal, the monarch of the state of Bharatpur, agreed to form a consortium with Safdargunj, the Mughal Wazir, against the Mughal Emperor. At the request of Imad-ul-Mulk (grand Wazir of the Mughal Empire), Raghunath Rao, younger brother of Balaji, sent a force headed by Malhar Rao Holkar to Bharatpur to make them retaliate. Suraj Mal proposed to offer Raghunath Rao a hefty sum of money to shield him from the attack. However, this offer was turned down, and later the fort of Kunher in Bharatpur was besieged in 1754 for four months. With the adulteration of Mughal intervention, the relations between Jatts and Marathas worsened.

Balaji Baji Rao had commendable diplomacy skills. Based on these skills, he established amicable relations with the Mughals to such an extent that they preordained him as the Deputy Governor of Malwa. The alliance of the Marathas and Mughals was witnessing unprecedented growth when Balaji Rao pledged to be loyal to the Mughal emperor and offered to provide them with Marathas soldiers as and when needed. He also aided Safdargunj and shielded him against the consortium of his hostiles, namely Javed Khan and the Nizam of Hyderabad, Nasir Jung.

Meanwhile, the Afghan King, Ahmad Shah Durrani, emerged from the Mughaliya Sultanate, crumbling them into pieces. To counter them, Mughals approached Balaji Baji Rao, who triumphantly pushed back the Durranis and received the power to collect tax from Lahore, Multan, and Sindh. Mughals took this victory to their advantage. To please the Durranis, the Emperor also gave the regions of Lahore and Multan to Ahmed Shah. This led to the advent of tension between the Durranis and the Marathas

Chapter 34

Dattaji Shinde

"Bachenge To Aur Bhi Ladenge"

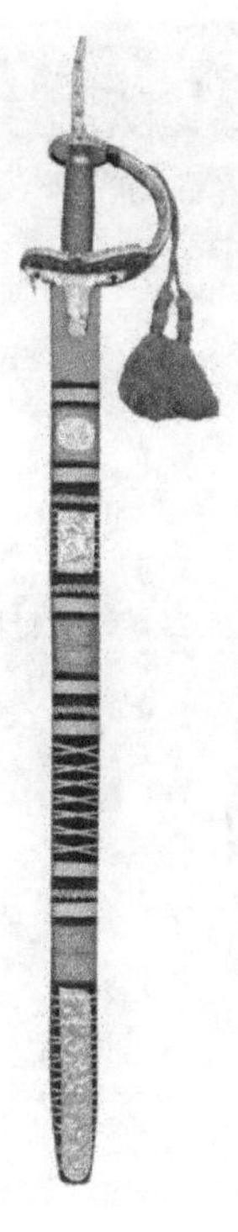

Dattaji Shinde was the elder brother of Mahadji Shinde. He was a Maratha General and commanded the Punjab region during Maratha and Afghan conflicts from 1758 to 1760. He was a loyal and daring soldier. When the danger of Abdali arose, it was Raghunathrao who asked Peshwa to send Dattaji Shinde to Delhi. He believed the only warrior like Dattaji can give an excellent fight to Afghans.

When the Maratha rule extended in Lahore, Peshwa assigned Dattaji Shinde to take care of other affairs of Northern *Hindustan*. In 1758 when Dattaji reached Delhi with many agendas in his charter, few were defeating Najib Khan, controlling burdens on the Maratha treasury, and bringing Delhi under control.

Shortly, Dattaji was able to control Delhi's affairs and designated his deputy to take care of Punjab. He then moved towards the east to take on Najib Khan. Within a few months, Dattaji received the SOS that Ahmad Shah Abdali, king of Afghanistan tried for his fifth invasion from West India. Dattaji decided to prevent Abdali from entering Delhi. He traveled back to Delhi and camped there to stop Afghans from entering Delhi.

On the fateful day of 10th January 1760, Rohillas of Najib Khan attempted to cross Barari Ghat to enter Delhi. Dattaji Shinde rushed to Barari Ghat from his camp to stop the intrusion of the enemies. Marathas fought bravely against Afghans. However, during the battle, Dattaji was shot down by a bullet, and he fell from the horse. He was lying there and was severely injured. Najib Khan Rohilla's counselor Qutub Shah saw Dattaji Shinde. He stepped down from his elephant, went near Dattaji, took his sword, and pierced Dattaji's body; he was bleeding and was in pain.

Qutub Shah asked with arrogance, *"Kyon Patilji, Humare Saath tum aur bhi ladoge?"* ("Hey Patilji, will you fight with us more?.

Even in severe pain, Dattaji replied, *"Bachenge toh aur bhi ladenge"* ("If I survive, will fight more")

Furious, Qutub Shah pulled his sword and beheaded Dattaji.

Dattaji was overpowered and murdered in battle with Afghans at Barari Ghat. This defeat was a turning point in Indian history which opened the way to the Afghan occupation of Delhi.

Chapter 35

"Third Battle Of Panipat-1761"

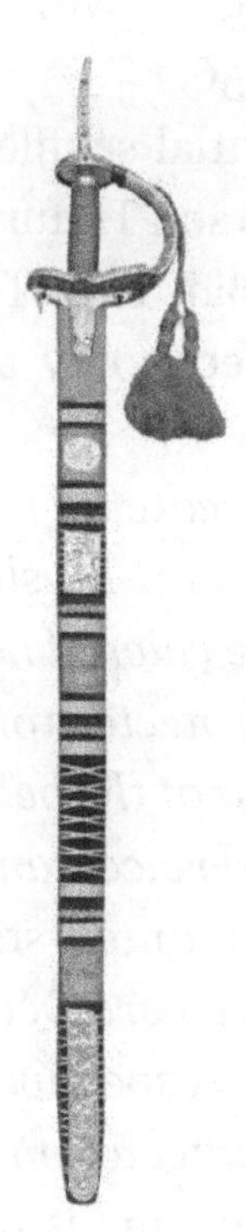

The 1760 decade housed one of the most devastating wars for the Maratha empire, the Third Battle of Panipat, which led to the quick disintegration of the Maratha legacy, power, and influence. Towards the later parts of the 1750s, Balaji Baji Rao had managed to bury all brawls with the Rajputs, keeping the situation of the Marathas with Durranis in mind. A peace treaty was signed with Dattaji Rao Scindia despite internally sour relations in 1756.

A series of consequential scuffles and political clashes with Ahmad Shah Durrani and his son Timur Shah Durrani had escalated during the reigns of Balaji Baji Rao. These preceded the battle of Panipat and worsened the economy and cavalry strength of the Marathas.

First of all, let's not create an image that the third battle of Panipat was the battle of Hindu-Muslim. This war was all about who will become the ultimate ruler of northwest India. During that period, Marathas were the protectors of the Mughal throne in Delhi. Maratha forces were fighting at the behest of Wazir of Delhi. Najib Khan, who was a Mughal serviceman, later joined Ahmad Shah Abdali to attack Delhi. He wanted status the same as Maratha because he believed Maratha were Deccan powers and don't have rights to rule North India. Irrespective of religions, history shows there has been a constant conflict to control Delhi by many rulers.

January 1761 had events in history that were so massive that they impacted the next 150 years of India. To know what led to the Battle of Panipat, we need to go two decades back. In 1740 when Nadir Shah from Iran invaded Northern India, Marathas realized the strategic importance of Punjab. During the same period, Marathas were involved in fighting in South Karnataka and the Nizam in Aurangabad. These battles were comfortable to manage for Marathas as both were near to Maharashtra. However, in the next decade, during the 1750s, they started stretching the battles far from

Maharashtra.

Maratha decided to take on Ahmed Shah Abdali, who was the King of Afghanistan. This was a decisive movement of Indian history, with India's entire political and power situation was about to change. Marathas had a plan to defeat Abdali and move towards Bengal and reduce the British force, another threat to the Maratha empire.

Marathas started their campaign to fight Abdali. However, many policy blunders were made by the Maratha empire in the preceding years, which resulted in internal fights with Rajputs. Sikhs from Punjab were supportive towards Maratha, however overoptimistic Marathas ignored them at that time. Thus, when the battle of Panipat started 1000 miles from their home base, they found themselves companionless. During the campaign, when Marathas took shelter in fort of Panipat. Ahmed Shah besieged the fort of Panipat, the Marathas were left with hardly any resources or explosives to either survive within the fort or go on an aggressive offensive. They stood still as they waited for Balaji Baji Rao's reinforcements to save the day; however, their cavalry could not make it beyond river Narmada. This forced the already helpless and starving Marathas to step out and take a chance at their lives, fight like the warriors they were known to be, instead of hiding inside, shamefully defeated.

Maratha loyalists like Malharrao Holkar and Mahadji Sindia took the war as lost. They moved away towards Delhi with small troops. Sadashiv Rao Bhau fought the battle till his last breath. The outcome of the battle was a massacre of those who had surrendered. Thousands of men were beheaded. Many thousand women were taken, imprisoned, and handed over to the military personnel.

The Jats of Bharatpur offered the Maratha'saccommo-dation during this time. In early February, Balaji Baji Rao Peshwa reached near Jhansi when Ahmad Shah Abdali was in control of Delhi. Abdali sent his emissary to negotiate a concord with the Peshwa. However, no treaty of peace was signed then. In March, Abdali hastily left Delhi as he could not manage his troop's monetary demands.

The Battle of Panipat induced heavy losses to the Marathas due to in decisive action to postpone the maneuver, ending with them being subdued. The conniving defeat in the battle came a severe blow to Balaji Baji Rao, who failed to provide reinforcement and lost his son and Sadashiv Rao in the process. He subsequently died in the same year, leaving a battering Maratha legacy behind for young Madhav Rao.

Chapter 36
Balwantrao Mehendele
"Loss Before Battle Of Panipat"

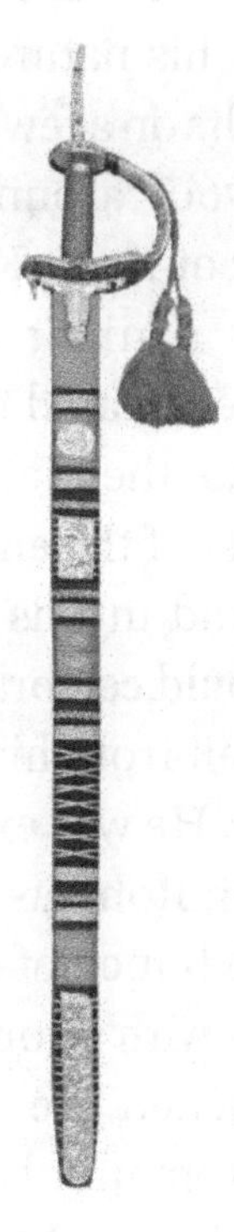

Balwantrao Mehendele was a close associate of Peshwa Balaji Rao and Sadashivrao Bhau, son of Chimaji Appa. He accompanied both in many expeditions in the south. When Peshwa Balaji Rao chose Sadhashivrao Bhau to lead the Panipat Campaign, Balwantrao joined Sadhashivrao. This was the first North campaign for both Sadhashivrao and Balwantrao.

As per a few scholars and historians, Balwantrao was hot-headed and arrogant. Due to his nature, many attacks of Marathas could not get the desired results on a few occasions.

On 7th December 1760, around a month before Panipat Battle, Sultan Khan (brother of Najib Khan) and the Rohillas army attacked Marathas. It was a night attack, and Rohillas took advantage of darkness and penetrated till Maratha trenches. Under the leadership of Balwant Rao, the Maratha army counter-attacked Afghans and slaughtered most of the enemies. Afghans were droved back by Maratha warriors, and in this attack, many Rohillas were killed. But before Maratha could celebrate the victory, one bullet hit Balwantrao's chest, and he fell from his horse. He was lying on the ground, injured but still alive. He was exposed to Rohillas, who were scattered and escaping. When Rohillas saw Maratha General fallen on the ground and injured. A bunch of Rohillas crowed Balwantrao and started slashing his body with swords. When Marathas grasped the act of Rohillas, they reached the spot where Balwantrao was fallen and rescued his body from mutilation. Even though Marathas saved Balwantrao's body but they could not save his life.

This was a significant blow for Marathas; Sadashivrao Bhau was deeply saddened by the loss of his trusted warrior. Had Balwantrao lived till the battle of Panipat, he could have contributed more to the Maratha army.

Chapter 37
Ibrahim Khan Gardi
"Artillery General Of Maratha"

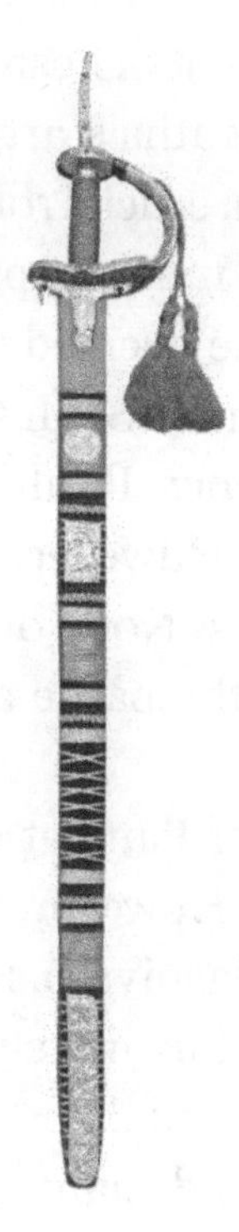

As I mentioned earlier, the third war of Panipat was not a war of any religion. Ibrahim Khan Gardi, part of the Maratha army during the battle, is one such example.

Ibraham Khan Gardi was expert artillery who served Nizam of Hyderabad. He was part of the Nizam army and participated in the battle of Palakhed against the Marathas. This battle was won by Marathas. Later Sadashivrao Bhau took Ibrahim under the Maratha army and gave sole management of Peshwa's artillery to him. In 1760 Ibrahim Khan Gardi led Maratha's artillery in the battle of Udgir against Nizam Ali. He played a crucial role in Maratha's victory.

Sadashivrao was very much impressed with the bravery and skills of Ibraham Khan. So, he decided to take Ibraham Khan in the Panipat campaign against Ahmad Shah Abdali.

Abdali tried to influence Ibraham Gardi to join the Afgan army in the name of religion. However, Gardi declined the offer and remained loyal to his masters. None of his 8,000 artillery soldiers decamped to Abdali during the battle and fought with uncommon valor.

When the third war of Panipat ended, Ahmad Shah Abdali emerged as a virtual winner. However, Marathas lost many of their brave warriors, including Sadashivrao. Ibraham Khan did maximum damage to Abdali's army. Unfortunately, he was caught alive by the Afgan army and was killed by Abdali.

Ironically, we don't find many details about Ibrahim Khan Gardi in our textbooks.

Chapter 38
Madhav Rao
"The Maratha Renaissance"

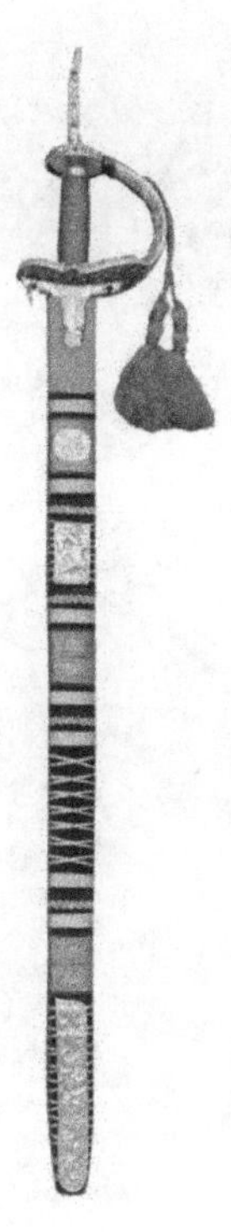

Under the leadership of Madhav Rao, the younger son of Balaji Rao, great historians accounted to see the spirits of Baji Rao I. He was a formidable warrior, just like his grandfather.

Most enemy forces had imagined the Marathas crumbled due to internally hollow relations and externally defeated wars like Panipat. Madhav Rao overturned the scenario into what came to be known as the Maratha Renaissance, or the Maratha rise from the dead.

Madhav Rao was the ninth Peshwa of the Maratha empire and played a crucial role in revitalizing Maratha supremacy post battle of Panipat. He wanted revenge for Panipat. In 1769, he sent a Maratha army in the northern expedition under Visaji Krishna Biniwala under the guidance of Tukoji Holkar and Mahadji Scindia. The Maratha army swept across the north, proclaiming their authority over the Rajputs and the Jats. Marathas moved further and defeated Rohillas. Rohilla Chief Zabita Khan, who was the son of Najib Ud Daullah, flew away under the terror of Marathas. Later he returned by paying a ransom demanded by Marathas in return for lost territory.

Peshwa Madhav Rao was constantly at odds with his uncle Raghunath Rao. This was openly reflected in the conflicts, coup attempts, and finally, the full-blown battle of Rakshabhuvan between the two relatives. However, Madhav Rao improved relations and fought battles with his loyal Nana Fadnavis, Gopalrao Patwardhan, Ramshastri Prabhune, and Tryambakrao Mama Pethe. One such alliance that he worked on was that with the Nizams. This politically brilliant decision helped them when the Marathas marched to Delhi, another reminiscence of his grandfather. The latter dared to threaten the Mughals on their throne.

One of the significant external conflicts during the time of

Madhav Rao was his battle with Hyder Ali. Raghunathrao, feeling threatened by Madhav Rao's indelible esteem and power, decided to go against his wish of assistance to sign a treaty with Hyder Ali. In two different attacks, the Marathas could not reach a conclusion in Mysore and conquer Hyder Ali. In 1670 they launched a third attack; however, Madhav Rao's tuberculosis became more substantial, and the Maratha Peshwa weaker. Finally, in 1772, this venerated Peshwa succumbed to the disease and left the succession of the Empire to Narayanrao, the younger brother of Madhav Rao.

Soon as Narayanrao took control, within a year, in 1773, he was murdered by Raghunathrao's ardent followers. This emerged to be a success for Raghunathrao. He finally ascended the throne of Peshwa in 1773. However, he could only be on the throne for two years. In 1775 he was overthrown from Pewshaship by the loyal courtiers of Narayanrao. Courtiers installed Narayanrao's son, Madhav Rao II, on the throne as the eleventh Maratha Peshwa.

Chapter 39
Nana Phadnis
"The Maratha Machiavelli"

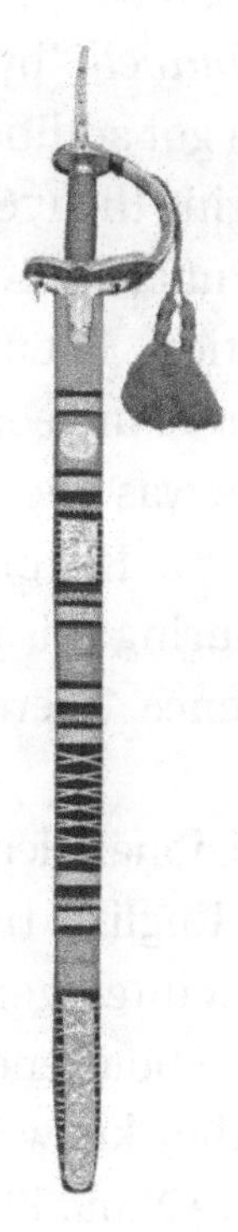

Balaji Janardhan Bhau was born on 12th February 1742 at Satara; his nickname was "Nana." Later he was famously known as Nana Phadnis. Once his grandfather saved the life of Balaji Vishwanath Peshwa, since then, both Peshwas and Phadnis's family had a cordial relationship and were like family. Nana was family to Peshwas. Based on trust and belief, Nana was made Phadnis means Finance minister for Peshwas. He was called *"Maratha Machiavelli"* by the Europeans.

Over the period, Nana got additional responsibilities, and he was part of Maratha army during the 1761 Panipat battle. He escaped from Panipat and reached Pune; he achieved great heights of the Maratha empire administration. Even though he was not a field soldier, he played a decisive role in keeping the Maratha pride high post the battle of Panipat. He was one of the known persons of the Maratha empire post-1761 era. He played a role in holding the Maratha alliances together during this phase when the British East India company grew its influence. There were a lot of inner conflicts within the Maratha alliance.

Nana Phadnis was a visionary leader and knew real threats to Marathas were French and English traders. Considering this, he created one of the most robust intelligence and spy networks, which helped him gain information about enemy moves. He was the real threat to the Britishers, and they knew this very well. Hence several attempts were made to remove Nana Phadnis from his position, but they failed miserably.

In 1772 when Madhavrao was dead, his brother Narayanrao became the Peshwa, however as part of internal conflicts, he was killed in 1773. After the death of Narayanrao, it was Nana's strategy to make Narayanrao's son (newborn) the next Peshwa. Nana was the head of the Barabhai Council, the alliance of influential Maratha Sardars and influencers for the Maratha empire.

A newborn baby was named "Sawai Madhavrao." Under the

decision of the *Barabhai* council, the newborn baby was declared as a new Peshwa to be ruled under Nana's supervision. On the other hand, the *Barabhai* council opposed Raghunath Rao (brother of Peshwa Balaji Baji Rao and uncle of Madhavrao and Narayanrao) to become the next Peshwa.

With the 40 days old son of Narayanrao, Madhav Rao II was conferred as the next Peshwa. The Maratha Empire's effective control was passed over to Nana Phadnis, the regent. Under his leadership and high-ranking court men like Mahadji Shinde, the Marathas defended their Empire fully against the British.

The Anglo Maratha wars were a result of the policy of warfare between two solid political forces. The pursuit of supremacy over the land of the Indian sub-continent by the East India Company was at the core of the trilogy of the Anglo Maratha conflicts.

The struggle of the Marathas, who were not ready to give up their motherland to the invading Britishers, commenced during the late 18th century. This struggle started between Marathas and Britishers with the onset of the first Anglo Maratha war. The confrontation lasted until the 19th century when the fearless Marathas warriors were defeated by the East India Company during decades-long combat's third and final episode.

First Anglo Maratha War (1775 – 1782)

Background to the war involved Raghunathrao signing the treaty of Surat but the British Calcutta Council condemning and annulling it with the treaty of Purandhar.

The first Anglo Maratha war was instigated when Nana Phadnis, head of the twelve Marathas Chiefs, permitted the French a port on the West Coast. This was evidently ultra vires of the treaty of Purandhar. Further developments ensued a planned attack by the Britishers on Pune. They were retaliated in Wadgaon by the Maratha troops led by Mahadji Shinde. Maratha won this battle against the

Britishers. The Britishers had no alternative but to sign the Treaty of Wadgaon and Treaty of Salbai, which concluded the first Anglo Maratha War in favor of the Marathas.

Till Nana was alive, he successfully defeated Britishers and kept them under the Maratha's supremacy. Unfortunately, Nana passed away in 1800, with the glory of the Maratha empire started fading. He will be remembered for rebuilding the pride of Marathas, primarily the post-battle of Panipat debacle in 1761.

Chapter 40
Mahadji Shinde
"Maratha Ruler In The State Of Gwalior"

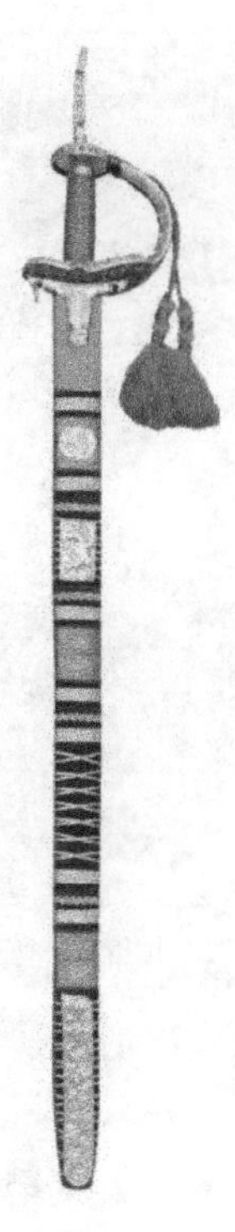

Mahadji Shinde was born on 3rd December 1730 and was the youngest son of Sardar Ranoji Rao Scindia. He became a respected name 'from the Sutlej to the Narmada.' He was the deputy of the Peshwa and eventually became the Maratha ruler in the state of Gwalior. After the battle of Panipat in 1761, when everyone thought the Maratha empire would perish, Mahadji Shinde, Madhav Rao I, and Nana Fadnavis brought back the Maratha empire on track. During Mahadji's reign, Maratha empire became one of the leading military power in India; with his leadership skills. He was the man behind helping Shah Alam II re-establish the Mughal empire in Delhi; however, Mughal was under Marathas in Delhi.

Mahadji Shinde was a part of the Maratha army in the Battle of Panipat; he was severely injured and was rescued later.

Even though in 1761 third battle of Panipat significantly weakened the Marathas, later in 1771 - 72, Marathas won Delhi. Mahadji Shinde kept the Mughal Emperor purely as a dummy. Mahadji was *Vakil-ul-Mutlaq* (Regent of Mughal affairs) and *Amir-ul-umara* (Head of the Amirs). Mahadji could sit at Delhi's throne himself and ruled, but he did not.

Mahadji Shinde played a pivotal role in defeating the British in the first Anglo-Maratha War. Having taken down the British in the first Anglo Maratha wars, their spirits were high with patriotism. Accordingly, the Marathas strove to further keep external powers away from their motherland. Meanwhile, Mahadji Shinde, one of the most loyal statesmen who served the Maratha Empire for over 60 years, played a significant role in expanding and maintaining powers and contributing to the resurrection of Peshwa Madhav Rao I. His role in the first anglo-Maratha war was conspicuous. He also played exemplary diplomacy when he managed to get the British to sign the Treaty of Wadgaon, Treaty of Salbai, and became the peacemaker between the British and the Peshwas.

In this decade, he went forward to expand his Empire to the Rajputana. The Marathas had teetering relation with Rajputs, changing as per the rulers and alliances. His first attempt to invade the region was thwarted in Lalsot in 1787. However, it was only to be followed by two staggering victories and taking over powerful kingdoms of Jodhpur and Jaipur in the Battles of Patan and Merta in 1790.

Mahadji Shinde was loyal to his alliances. He was also credited with defeating Mohmad Shah Abdali from Lahore.

Chapter 41
Rana Khan
"Bhai"

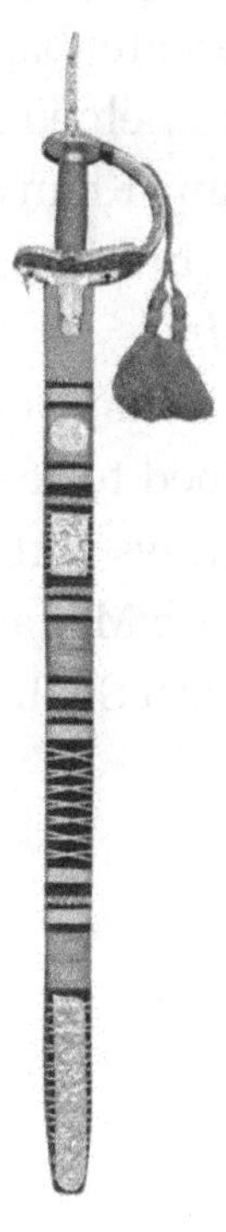

Mahadji Scindia fought bravely against his enemies and was responsible for reinitiating Mughal emperor Shah Alam in Delhi. He was a part of the Maratha military during the third Battle of Panipat. During the war, he was severely wounded and was vulnerable to get killed by the Afgan army. For his rescue came Rana Khan, who was a water carrier. Rana Khan carried Mahadji from the Battlefield by hiding him inside the water holding a water bag made of leather.

Rana Khan nursed and helped Mahadji to recover and took him to Pune. Mahadji kept Rana Khan along with him for the rest of his life and treated him like his brother. Mahadji honored Rana Khan with the title "Rana Khan *Bhai*."

Mahadji Scindia later became one of the greatest warriors of the Maratha Empire and helped to re-establish the lost prestige of Marathas. Rana Khan was always with Mahadji Shinde during this journey, and in 1790 he was with Mahadji at Red Fort when Mahadji got Sanads from Mughal emperor Shah Alam.

Chapter 42
Yashwantrao Holkar
"The Chakravarti"

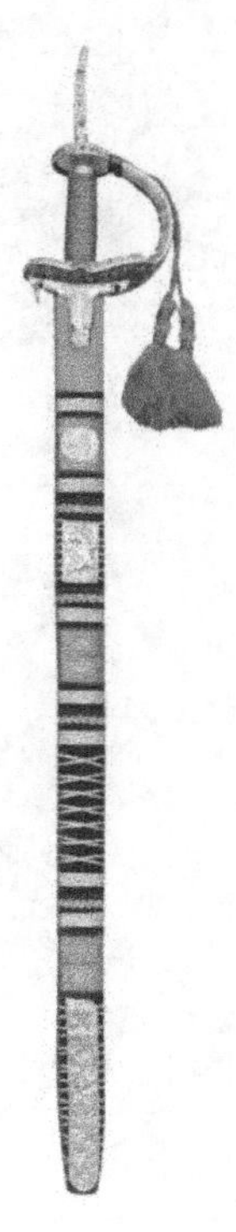

The decade 1790 began with the unfortunate demise of Mahadji Shinde in 1794 when he was at the hilt of his career in the Maratha Confederacy. He had established unparalleled power and influence that he left behind for Daulat Rao Scindia in 1794. Unfortunately, Mahadji Shinde had no heir. Daulat Rao was the grandson of Mahadji's elder brother Tukoji Rao Scindia. With Madhavrao II committing suicide under the immense pressure of not matching up to Nana Fadnavis's authority, Raghunathrao's son Baji Rao II assumed power as the next Peshwa of the Marathas. Under the leadership of Baji Rao II and the Scindias, another high-ranking chief general created an impactful difference in the struggle of the confederacy against the British.

After 1795, the downward spiral of Marathas started. After post deaths of Mahadji Shinde, Nana Fadanvis, there was a leadership vacuum in the Maratha Empire. During this time, a new leader emerged in the Maratha empire, and he was Yashwantrao Holkar. He belonged to the Holkar dynasty of the Maratha empire. The rising power of Yashwantrao had started threatening Daulat Rao Scindia, who was under improper external influence and was being instigated against his own. As a result, the Empire was confused with no heir to Madhavrao, and two emerging powers, the Scindias and the Holkars took charge. On 14th September 1797, Daulat Scindia attacked Yashwant Rao; however, he managed to escape. After that, series of attempts were made to arrest Yashwantrao, but he escaped successfully. The enmity between the two powers was strengthened by 1798.

Emerging from the Holkar dynasty of the Maratha empire, Yashwantrao Holkar was crowned as the King or Raja in 1799. After taking over the succession in Indore, Yashwantrao Holkar captured Ujjain by defeating Scindia in the Battle of Ujjain in 1801. By May 1802, Maharaja Yashwantrao Holkar was already marching towards Pune to conquer Sendhwa, Chalisga, Dhulia, Malegaon, Gardond,

Pandharpur, Kurkumbh, and many other territories. On 25th October 1802, in the Battle of Poona, Yashwant Rao Holkar defeated the combined forces of Scindias and the Peshwa at Hadapsar. Intimidated by Holkar's increasing power, the Peshwa fled, and Holkar let them, despite the chance of capturing them.

After conquering Pune, Yashwantrao Holkar took the reigns of the Marathas in his hands and installed Amrutrao, adopted son of Peshwa Raghunath Rao, as the Peshwa. In 1803, he reinstated the powers of Baji Rao II and officially declared him as the Peshwa. Daulat Rao Scindia decided to join hands with Holkar to take down the increasing menace of the British. However, Yashwantrao later realized it was just an alliance of convenience. Yashwantrao soon realized that most Maratha dynasties had signed treaties of compliance with the British; disappointed with the combination of reasons, he decided to return to Indore in 1804.

He continued his battle against the British and refused to give in like others. Yashwantrao Holkar appealed to the Indian kings to join him in the fight against the British. His statement, "First country and then religion; we will have to rise above caste religion and our state in the interest of our country," caused a massive uproar and declared an open challenge against the British.

Chapter 43
Maratha Empire
"The Conclusion"

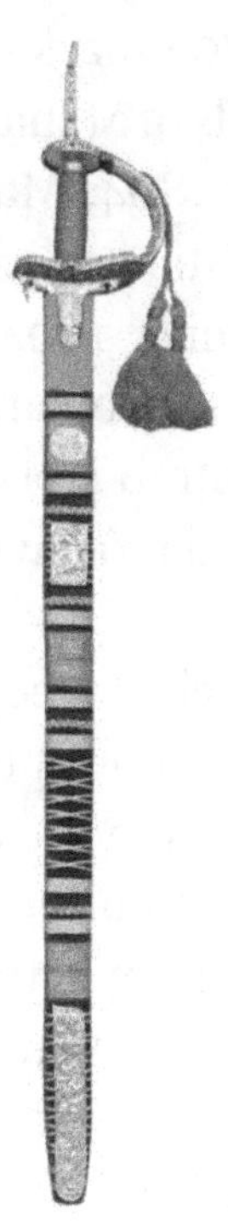

Having resolved to retrieve their princely states from the Britishers, the Marathas united, ready to make one last maneuver. On the other side, Britishers were suspecting that the Marathas were harboring the Pindaris to restore their power which they had robbed them of. Therefore, various Maratha chiefs Peshwa Baji Rao II, Malharrao Holkar, and Mudhoji II, stood united and set up an army against them.

June to September 1804 marked the defeat of the Britishers at different battles at the hands of Maharaj Holkar in Kunch, Leukan, and Kota. Then on 8th July 1804, Maharaja Yashwantrao Holkar defeated the army of Colonel Manson and Leukan at Mukundare and Kota. Finally, on 14th November 1804 in Farrukhabad, Lord Lake went to attack Yashwant Rao Holkar. Still, he remained a mute spectator, watching Yashwantrao Holkar proceed towards Deeg as he didn't dare attack Maharaja Yashwantrao Holkar and feared a brutal defeat.

Lord Lake finally attacked Deeg on 3rd January 1805. The successive siege of Bharatpur continued for three months and was equated with the war described in the epic Mahabharata. Although the Jat King Ranjit Singh had initially offered him support, he signed an agreement with the British on 17th April 1805. This was when Maratha had nearly won the war. Subsequently, Maharaja Yashwantrao Holkar had to leave Bharatpur.

The British Council asked Lord Lake to make concord with Yashwantrao Holkar. If they were too late, the other Indian kings would accept the request of Yashwantrao Holkar. It might result in a conclusive British defeat. The British decided, on 24th December, to sign a peace treaty with him. Post which the treaty of Rajghat was signed. As per the treaty, the British returned all his territory and affirmed that they would not interfere in any matters relating to the Holkars.

Besides Yashwant Rao's glorious rise and reign, two

significant battles were fought under the leadership of Peshwa Baji Rao II.

Holkar defeated the combined forces of Scindia and Peshwas in 1802. Post this, Baji Rao II sought British refuge, much like his father, Raghunathrao, consequently signed the suicide treaty of the Maratha Empire, the treaty of Bassein. By all means, with this treaty, Baji Rao II gave all his freedom to the British. With the treaty coming into effect, Baji Rao II no longer make any alliance with Holkars and Scindias without permission from British authorities. It was a shocking act for Shinde, Holkar, Bhonsles, who were part of the Maratha Empire. They all knew this treaty can lead the British to take control of their territories soon. However, even after knowing the danger from British power, Maratha alliance could not unite against the British. Due to internal quarrels, Holkar moved out of Scindia and Bhosale Alliance. Seeing this as an opportunity and treaty of Bassein favoring them, the British declared war against Scindia and Bhosale. This was the beginning of the second Anglo Maratha war, which was won by the Britishers.

This treaty declared Marathas ceding most territories to the British, acting as mere subsidiaries with hardly any power. They also asked for control over foreign affairs, and the East India Company troops were permanently stationed at Pune. The other Maratha chiefs objected to the treaty as it was fatal for independent Maratha states. Soon, Ahmednagar was captured by the British, and the Battles of Argaon and Gawilghur were lost by the Marathas.

The Second Anglo Maratha war was fought between 1803 and 1805 that ultimately resulted in the victory of the Britishers against the Maratha-Holkar faction. As the Anglo Maratha war began, the Scindias and Bhonsales were struggling to resist the British. The Battle of Assaye broke out as Major Arthur Wellessly struck at the combined army of Daulat Scindia and Raja of Bera. Marathas gave a tough competition to the British army. They showed tremendous grit and courage on the battlefield. However, they lacked an able leader like Wellesley. The soldiers of the Maratha Army were not well trained, and the Maratha themselves lacked unity which led to a pivotal defeat in the more enormous loss that followed.

As it was the final attempt to overthrow external powers and undo the wrongs, Holkars joined the war later. The result was a mediation to make peace. Thus, the British victory in the second Anglo Maratha war was marked as a crucial moment in the colonial suppression of the Indian subcontinent.

Background To The Third Anglo Maratha War

With most powers snatched away by the English, Marathas had started facing other problems like economic crunch and an apparent lack of superior leadership. Then, in 1810, a financial feud between the Peshwas and Gaekwads caught British attention. Intending to scrape away whatever was left of the Empire, the British forced the Marathas to sign the treaty of Poona. Claiming an end to the revenue collection from the Gaekwads and ceding of major territories to the British.

Under the leadership of Peshwa Baji Rao II, Marathas lacked more than just valiance and strategic planning. It lacked ethics and diplomacy, which led to treacheries and conflicts between the integral powers of the Empire among dynasties. Moreover, they lacked military equipment and sufficient training to defend themselves against the British's progressive forces and progressive artillery.

The Maratha Empire Meets Its End (1814- 1818)

Consistent demeaning defeats and embezzled powers by the British indicated the definite doom of the Maratha empire. Baji Rao II acted recklessly and brought the Marathas the final war that disintegrated the Marathas with a final blow with desperation and powers starving temperament.

The overbearing nature of the British irritated the Maratha chiefs. It instigated Baji Rao II, whose measures of conducting raids through the Pindaris sparked off the third Anglo Maratha war at Khadki in 1817. The Peshwa felt suffocated under the restriction placed on him by the British, so he began to use the remaining of his accumulated treasures to augment his army. By November 5th, he sent large bodies of his army towards British residency. Mountstuart Elphinstone, the British officer, got an inkling of it, and in the nick of time, he left the British habitation and escaped to Khadki.

The British residency was charred down, and it was marked as the first declaration of the third Anglo Maratha War. Soon the Maratha army spread over up to Ganesh Khind. The battle was fought vigorously, but unfortunately, a ditch on the plane broke Maratha's first charge. After that, sedition by one of Baji Rao II's chief Sardar Ghorpade Sondurkar, ruined the Marathas of any chances to win.

British forces formed a surrounded square and killed Moro Dixit (Peshwa's Minister) and his troops. Soon Marathas retired from the field, leaving behind their heavy artillery. The Battle of Khadki was subsequently followed by the Battle of Koregaon sparked when Baji Rao II captured the Chakan fort from the British. Then, on 1st January 1818, Baji Rao II led 28,000 cavalrymen to attack Pune with the last hopes of taking down the British from the Deccan. This was an intuitive action before the British attacked the Marathas. However, despite outnumbering their troops in Pune, the Marathas withdrew, hesitant of the possible failure and loss of life that the eminent British reinforc-ements would have caused.

Despite the withdrawal, the battle of Koregaon came to be known as a hugely celebrated one in Maratha history. This is because this was one of the last battles of Marathas that deeply inflicted casualties on the British in physical and moral terms.

Later, Peshwa Baji Rao II tried to obtain the support of Scindias and Holkars. Still, they were entirely restricted by British control in the form of signed treaties. In the end, Peshawa Baji Rao II surrendered to John Malcolm on June 3rd, 1818. He was dethroned and was exiled off to Bithoor. Thus, officially ending the Maratha empire supremacy.

Chapter 44
Maratha Empire
"The Pride Of Ancient India"

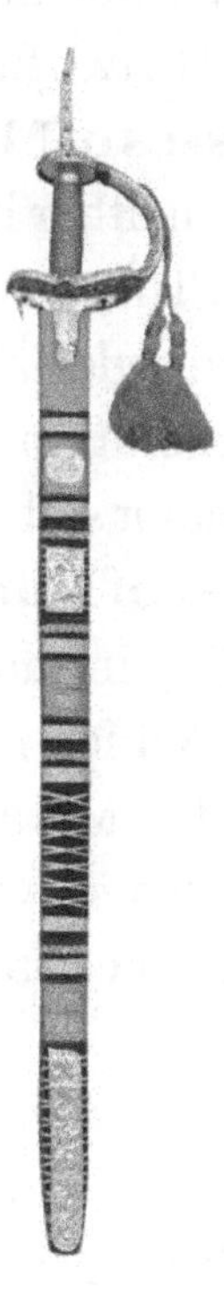

An empire that took pride in its warriors, resilient and valiant like never seen before, disintegrated within two decades. Marathas played a pivotal role in freeing India of external powers and, to a great extent, successfully weakened the Mughals and gained control over their dominance. Then what led to such absolute defeat at the hands of the East India Company who had only started as an influential business operator?

The cause can be traced to two fundamental factors:

1.Internal Weaknesses of Marathas

Shivaji was an idealist; neither he nor his colleagues paid any attention to self-gain or glory. They fought selflessly for "*Swarajya*" but soon, idealism fell from the pedestal, and self-interest took place. The conflicts between the federation of five Maratha chiefs rose; hence, disunity proved their major setback.

2. Military Weakness of Marathas

Mughals had been ruling in India for centuries before being confronted by the Marathas. Which meant most artillery and war equipment were similar, and the Marathas were familiar with their war tactics. However, with Britishers, who came from entirely different continent brought advanced technologies and skills that the Marathas couldn't stand against.

Centuries of domination by external powers in the Indian subcontinent witnessed and recorded Marathas as the sole power that rose to match and occlude the Mughals. With Shivaji's rebellion and regulations being passed on as a legacy laced with nationalism and patriotism, Marathas became undefeatable for most of their reign. So much so that even the records of the enemies that fought them sing praises of them. Enemies believed that Marathas produced the most remarkable rulers, whether in the form of Chhatrapatis or Peshwas, that they had ever come across.

Shivaji's life lessons are so influential that they can transform us to achieve seemingly impossible tasks when invoked. Maratha

Empire, founded by Shivaji Maharaj, was indeed an elite one due to a few of the below factors-

1. More than the territorial victory greatness of the Maratha empire lies in its ideological victory. Mughal empire was at its zenith when Shivaji Maharaj was crowned king of the Maratha empire and ruled the kingdom as a sovereign ruler. This was evident that the Mughals were not the de facto ruler of the complete Indian mainland even at their peak.
2. From the beginning, they had a brilliant intelligence team lead by capable leaders. This helped Marathas to get crucial information about their enemies. Moreover, Marathas always had an eye on Enemies movement, giving them the advantage of planning attacks.
3. Under the leadership of Peshwa Bajirao, Maratha empire ruled almost 70% of current India. Their rule stretched till Peshawar and Attock. At their peak, Marathas ruled from the current Tanjavur in Tamil Nadu to Attock, Pakistan.
4. Since Sahu Maharaj took a position as Chattrapati, the Mughal Emperor was under Maratha's protection until Marathas were defeated by the East India Company.

Jai Bhavani Jai Shivaji

References

- *"The Founding Of Maratha Freedom" by S. R. Sharma*
- *"Shivaji The Portrait Of A Patriot" V.B.Kulkarni*
- *History of the Marathas by R. S. Chaurasia)*
- *"Shivaji: The Founder Of Maratha Swaraj" by C V Vaidya*
- *"Shivaji And His Times" by Jadunath Sarkar*
- *Maratha Confederacy - A Study In Its Origin And Development by V. S. Kadam*
- *Rise Of The Peshwas by H. N. Sinha*
- *Baji Rao I The Great Peshwa by C. K. Srinivasan*
- *Nana Phadnis and The External Affairs Of The Maratha Empire by Y. N. Deodhar*
- *The Last Peshwa And The English Commissioners 1818-1851 by Pratul Gupta*
- *Baji Rao II And The East India Company 1796-1818 by Pratul Gupta*
- *Panipat 1761 by Shankar Shejwalkar*
- *Marathas And Panipat by Hari Ram Gupta*
- *Selections From The Satara Rajas And The Peshwas Diaries Viii by Kashinath Balkrishna Marathe*
- *Bombay And The Marathas by W. S. Desai*
- *Rise and Fall of The Maratha Empire 1750-1818 by Sanish Nandakumar*

I personally recommend you read the above books to get more insights into Maratha Empire.

You may also like....

"Ashtavakra - The Vedic Sage: Unusual Tales of Country Called Bharat" was the first published book by Author Gopish Gopalkrishna.

Who was the creator of Ashtavakra Gita?

What is Yudhishtra's Curse on Womanhood?

How first Naga Prathistta was created?

Why Hanuman turned red?

These are the few exciting tales you will read in this book, along with other stories. Bharat (India) is a beautiful country full of wonders and surprises. This country has many religions, languages, festivals, states, and unusual tales as well. This book collects 22 unique tales and the first book of the series, "The unusual tales of the country called Bharat." All these stories are different and not related to each other. Hence readers will get to know new tales in every chapter.

There is always something special about short stories, mainly mythological, as it always sticks to the traditional rules of the craft. However, these stories are vibrant and for all ages, from children to grandparents. This book is an effort to reach out to more readers and spread the stories of the great land Bharat.

Book is available on Amazon, Kindle, and Flipkart.

www.ingramcontent.com/pod-product-compliance
Lightning Source LLC
LaVergne TN
LVHW052007160826
845678LV00005B/1671

* 9 7 8 9 3 9 2 9 0 0 0 4 4 *